SPENDING TIME WITH THE LORD

— Expanded Edition —

by
Bill Freeman

First Edition 1990
Expanded Edition 1999

Library of Congress Catalog
Card Number: 98-67908

ISBN 0-914271-95-4

Ministry Publications

PO Box 28338
Scottsdale, AZ 85255
(800) 573-4105
Email: orders@thechristian.org

Printed in the United States of America

CONTENTS

Preface

This volume comprises spoken messages given between 1984 and 1998 in Seattle, Washington and Scottsdale, Arizona. All the messages were later printed in the monthly publication called *The Christian.* The main burden of these messages is focused on the preeminence of Christ and how it is related to our daily life.

First, this preeminence is seen in God's eternal purpose of transforming us into the image of His Son. This transforming work is accomplished by our learning to "behold the glory of the Lord" (2 Cor. 3:18). So it is vital in our daily life to spend quality time with the Lord, learning how to be in His presence beholding His glory.

Second, the preeminence of Christ is seen in our recognizing His voice as the good Shepherd (John 10:27). Learning the nature of His voice and how to be compatible with it will lead us into a life where Christ is our relationship with everything. In this way He will come to have the first place in all things.

Spending Time with the Lord is published with the desire and prayer that the Lord will use the reading of this volume to enrich your enjoyment and experience of spending time with Him in order that He would have the preeminence in all things.

— *Bill Freeman*
December 1999

Scripture quotations are taken from a combination of translations including *The New King James Version,*[†] *The King James Version, The New American Standard Version,*[§] etc. Minor changes have been made in the various versions from time to time to give a better rendering of the Hebrew and Greek texts.

Throughout the Scripture quotations, words are italicized for added emphasis.

"Mary...was seated at the Lord's feet and was listening to His Word...Mary has chosen the good part, which shall not be taken away from her."

❦ *Luke 10:39, 42*

1

The Need to Spend Time with the Lord

"I saw more clearly than ever that the first great and primary business to which I ought to attend every day was to have my soul happy in the Lord. The first thing to be concerned about was not how much I might serve the Lord, how I might glorify the Lord, but how I might get my soul into a happy state and how my inner man might be nourished."

– *George Müller*

The sense of need

The sense of need is always at the base of our making progress in the Christian life. This is a spiritual principle given to us by the Lord Jesus in Matthew 5:3, "Blessed are the poor in spirit, for theirs is the kingdom of heaven." To be poor in spirit means we sense our need for God, realizing we have absolutely nothing in ourselves. Accordingly, what often motivates us to spend more time with the Lord is an ever-deepening realization of our need of Him. Thus, the sense of need becomes the very factor of our spiritual progress — it causes us to seek Him and spend time with Him.

To be without a sense of need in our Christian life is a sure sign of spiritual decay. The Lord's diagnosis of the church in

Laodicea in Revelation 3:14-20 reveals that lukewarmness, pride, and self-sufficiency are all directly related to a lack of spending time with the Lord. He says to the Laodiceans, "Behold, I stand at the door and knock; if anyone hears My voice and opens the door, I will come in to him and dine with him and he with Me" (v. 20). In this verse, the Lord was virtually saying to them that they had not opened the door of their hearts to spend time with Him in fellowship. Yet it also shows us that He is patiently standing at the door and knocking, seeking to get His believers to find time to "dine" with Him.

The Greek verb *deipneo* (δειπνέω), translated "dine" or "sup" in Revelation 3:20, refers to the daily time that was set apart to eat the main meal. In Luke 14:17 it is called "the dinner hour." In other words, the Lord's supreme desire for us is that we would sense the need to have a daily "dinner hour," spending time with Him.

The need to be supplied

The very nature of the Christian life requires that we spend time with the Lord because the Christian life is a supplied life. It is a life that is supplied to us. It has nothing to do with our own resources or any potential in ourselves. It has everything to do with our opening up to Another life to be supplied by that life from beginning to end. The Christian life is a life that has been prepared for us and is then furnished to us by God. He intends to continually supply Himself to us. It is for this reason that we need to spend time with the Lord — to receive this supply.

Sometimes when we hear the truth from the Scriptures or from others, we may take it as a personal demand upon us and feel threatened with thoughts like, "I'm not like that. I could never do that." Or, "I can't imagine that I could ever feel that way. I just can't live up to that." When we have these kinds of thoughts and feelings, if we do not realize that the Christian life is a supplied life, we may conclude that this life is not for us and give up.

But listen to this — Every word that God has spoken in the Bible, whatever it is, whatever apparent demand it brings, God wants to supply that very thing into our being. It is not that we are expected to "measure up," or come up with the ability to perform in ourselves. No, God intends to continually supply Himself to us. We must understand the Christian life in this way — it is a supplied life. From beginning to end, it is supplied to us. And this supply comes to us and is dispensed into us in a very special and enjoyable way — *by spending time with the Lord.*

The penetrating words in Hebrews 4:12-13 tell us that the word of God divides soul and spirit, discerns the thoughts and intents of our heart, and lays us naked and bare before His eyes. These words are enough to sink one into despair. Yet these very words are specifically intended to bring us to Christ, our sympathizing High Priest, to receive our constant supply at the throne of grace (vv. 14-16). Being exposed in God's light is always a signal to us to once again draw our supply from Him. The Christian life is a life that has already been lived for us. Christ lived the life that God intended man to live. And now this life that has already been lived is *continuously* being supplied to us.

In the New Testament the Greek word *epichoregia* (ἐπιχορηγία) depicts the Christian life as a supplied life. For example, Philippians 1:19 says, "For I know that this shall turn to my salvation through your prayer, and *the bountiful supply (epichoregia)* of the Spirit of Jesus Christ." In the ancient Greek world the root word *choregia* was used to describe the person who was responsible for a chorus of singers or dancers. In brief, this person was responsible for supplying all the needs of all the members of the chorus. He was "the supplier." The Greek word meant that he was both a leader and a provider of all the needs of the chorus. Whether it was clothing, food, or money, he supplied everything; and he supplied it lavishly and abundantly without rationing or restriction.

Today this New Testament word for "supply" can be likened to being on a full scholarship as a university student. You are very relaxed. You are free from anxiety over your needs. You do not have to work your way through school; you just *receive* all the benefits of your scholarship. All your practical needs are cared for. Your tuition is cared for. Your research needs are cared for. Everything is fully supplied.

This is the thought behind the word *epichoregia*. When the apostle Paul applied this word to the Christian life, he was conveying that everything in the Christian life is provided for. The normal Christian life is like being on a full spiritual scholarship with everything supplied to us. Paul surely had this in mind when he declared in Ephesians 1:3, "Blessed be the God and Father of our Lord Jesus Christ, who has blessed us with *every spiritual blessing* in the heavenlies in Christ."

When you see your shortages and realize that you do not have a fervent love for the Lord — your heart is not inclined toward Him and His Word that much — God's desire at that point is to supply Himself to you. *He* wants to be your love for Him and that necessary desire for His Word. So never be troubled, never be fearful.

Every new juncture in our Christian life, no matter what it is, is simply another occasion for fresh supplies from the throne of grace. For example, if you are reacting toward your husband, what you need supplied to you is Christ lived out toward your husband. Or if you feel anxious about your financial situation, what you need supplied to you is a life of trusting the Lord, taking one day at a time, and seeking first the kingdom of God. For every kind of lack there is a supply of life waiting to meet it. You may be exposed to a sinful and worldly environment, and you need the power to resist temptation. The life that overcomes sin and the world will also be supplied to you.

We must continually realize that we are vessels receiving the bountiful supply of the Spirit of Jesus Christ. Our whole understanding of the Christian life must be renewed in this way. *The Christian life is a supplied life.* Thus, spending time with the Lord is prime time in our daily life to get connected with the supply.

The process of transformation

Spending time with the Lord not only supplies us to live our daily Christian life, but it is also the means for us to experience a transformation into the image of Christ Himself. From the moment we receive Christ and are regenerated, we are ushered into a lifelong *process* of transformation.

Second Corinthians 3:18 describes this process of being transformed into the image of Christ: "But we all, with unveiled face, beholding and reflecting as in a mirror the glory of the Lord, are being transformed into the same image from glory to glory, even as from the Lord Spirit."

By this process of transformation, our natural being undergoes a kind of "metabolic change." This means that a new element is replacing the old. Just as our eating and drinking cause our physical body to undergo a process of metabolism in which new elements enter our body and replace the old, so also our beholding the Lord causes our natural being to undergo a process of "spiritual metabolism." This means the faculties of our mind, emotion, and will receive a new element — Christ Himself — and are thereby transformed into His image. According to 2 Corinthians 3:18, this process takes place *while* we spend time beholding the glory of the Lord. By daily spending time with the Lord, we are putting ourselves in a position for transformation to take place.

Throughout the Bible we see God's purpose over our being. In *eternity past,* according to Romans 8:29, God predestinated us to be conformed to the image of His Son. In *creation,* according to Genesis 1:26-27, God made man in His own image. In *redemption,* according to Colossians 1:13-15, we have been transferred into the kingdom in which Christ is the image of the invisible God, the Firstborn of all creation. In our *daily life,* according to 2 Corinthians 3:18, we are existing to be transformed into the image of our glorified Lord. In *resurrection,* according to 1 Corinthians 15:49, we shall all one day bear the image of the heavenly. In *eternity future,* according to Revelation 22:4, we will be those who see His face and bear His image, even as it says, "His name shall be on their foreheads."

In light of God's revealed purpose in eternity past, in creation, in redemption, in daily life, in resurrection, and in eternity future, should we not spend time with Him for the fulfillment of this all-encompassing purpose? If we truly see that we are presently under the process of God's eternal purpose of transformation, we will be strongly motivated to spend time with the Lord for this to take place.

We are transformed into His image, not by self-effort or by imitation, but by spending time genuinely beholding Him. This kind of beholding requires that we set aside specific blocks of time regularly in which we, like Mary, cease from all other activities and preoccupations to give our undivided attention to behold Him (Luke 10:38-42).

The nature of transformation

The need for spending time with the Lord must also be considered from the viewpoint of the *nature* of transformation. The Greek verb *metamorphoo* (μεταμορφόω), translated "transformed" or "transfigured" is used exactly four times in the New Testament: in Matthew 17:2; Mark 9:2; Romans 12:2; and 2 Corinthians 3:18. Every time this word is used, without exception, it is in the *passive* voice. In Matthew 17:2 and Mark 9:2, when the Lord was on the mountain being "transfigured" or "transformed," on His part it was passive, that is, it happened to Him. In Romans 12:2, again the word "transformed" is in the passive voice: "Be transformed by the renewing of the mind." This means that our transformation is something happening *to* us. Finally, in 2 Corinthians 3:18, "being transformed" is also in the passive voice.

On our part, the nature of transformation is passive — it is something that happens to us. We, as the subject, are being acted upon, not doing the acting. For example, the statement "I am baptizing" is in the active voice (the subject is acting); whereas "I am being baptized" is in the passive voice (the subject is being acted upon). When we are beholding the glory of the Lord we are being acted upon — we are *being* transformed — by the Lord Spirit. This passive process of being transformed requires spending special time in the Lord's presence beholding Him.

The fact that the nature of transformation is passive reveals that there is no need to attempt to correct ourself, improve ourself, or change ourself in a religious way. Transformation is a process that happens to us. It is the spontaneous and automatic working of the Lord Spirit within us and upon us. For the Lord to be able to do this transforming work upon us, there is the need for us to spend time with Him, using our spirit to behold Him. So in our daily life we need to pay more attention to spending time with Him beholding His glory, rather than spending time being occupied with our own efforts and energy.

2

Beholding the Lord Requires Time

"To everything there is a season, and a time to every purpose under the sun." Eccl. 3:1

"This is literally true, there is a time for everything. Can it be true, as so many maintain, that there is no time for communion with God? Is not the most important matter for which we must find time, fellowship with God, in which we may experience His love and His power? Give God time, I beseech you. . . . Dear child of God, it is of little use to speak of the deeper, more abundant life of Christ as our life, if we do not daily, above all things, take time for intercourse with our Father in heaven. The life and love and holiness of God cannot be ours amidst the distractions and temptations of the world, unless we give God time to reveal Himself to us and to take possession of our hearts."

– Andrew Murray

Beholding and reflecting

The word "beholding" in 2 Corinthians 3:18 is used only one time in the entire New Testament and has no counterpart in the Old Testament. The depth of this Greek word is seen in its literal translation, which includes not only the activity of beholding but also that of reflecting. This means that we always reflect what we behold.

Let me give an example of beholding and reflecting. If a person spends hours watching television, eventually he begins to reflect the things he has been beholding. He starts thinking, feeling, and reacting according to what he has been looking at. Another example is reading novels. People who spend time reading novels actually begin to reflect what they read in their thinking. Beholding such things automatically affects your inner being. You cannot help but be involved in what you are reading and be influenced by it. Statistics indicate that crimes have occurred as a result of watching violence and immorality on television or reading about such things in novels.

Of course, the above examples illustrate the negative side. But we must see that the principle is the same on the positive side—what we behold is what we reflect. When we spend time with the Lord beholding Him we will automatically reflect Him. It is by this divinely-appointed way that we are being transformed into His image. We will spontaneously beam out Christ when we spend time beholding Him.

A lengthy period of time

Although the word *beholding* occurs only once in the Bible, the context of its occurrence in 2 Corinthians 3 supplies us with a full picture of what this beholding includes. To begin with, the background of the word *beholding* is found in

Exodus 33 and 34, which describes Moses' stay of forty days and forty nights with the Lord on Mount Sinai. At that time, Moses had taken the second set of stone tablets up to the mountain for the Lord to write the ten commandments upon them. Due to this lengthy period of time spent with God on the mountain, Moses came down not only with the tablets written upon, but also with the skin of his face shining with God's glory. He experienced a transformation as a result of spending a lengthy period of time with the Lord.

Paul identifies Moses' shining face as the glory of the old covenant ministry (2 Cor. 3:7, 9). Even though it was a passing glory, the old covenant ministry did have its glory. When Moses stayed on the mountain in God's presence for such a lengthy period of time, a transforming glory was infused into him. Because of the glory shining on Moses' face, he put a veil over it to cover the fading glory of the old covenant. But now, under the new covenant, whenever the heart turns to the Lord, the veil is taken away (2 Cor. 3:16). All the New Testament believers have an unveiled face so that they may behold the glory of the Lord.

Moses had prayed to the Lord in Exodus 33:18, "Please, show me Your glory." Then he spent time in God's glory with an unveiled face and he was changed (Exo. 34:34-35). In Deuteronomy 10:10 when Moses refers to his time with God, he says, "I stayed in the mountain." The original Hebrew word for *stayed* implies "I *lingered* in the mountain." This indicates that Moses realized the necessity of staying and even lingering with God on the mountain. Again, Exodus 33 and 34 provide the entire background of this one word *beholding*.

Thus, for us to know what this beholding is, we need to be impressed with Moses' stay with the Lord.

What stands out in Moses' experience of beholding the Lord and talking to Him, even face to face as an intimate friend (Exo. 33:11), is the time he spent—forty days and forty nights. It took this specific length of time for Moses to soak in the glory of God and to come down transformed. Of course, this transformation was only to the degree of the Old Testament glory. Nevertheless, there was a glory.

It is significant that Moses' record includes the amount of time he spent with the Lord on the mountain. This helps us to see that time is involved in the *beholding* in 2 Corinthians 3:18. We must realize that beholding the Lord to be transformed takes time. Being a person that makes time to be with the Lord is the sure way to be transformed into His image. Transformation does not happen superficially. It takes time. And not only so, it takes the right kind of time — quality time with the Lord in a proper way.

When Moses went up to the mountain, he took empty tablets. Therefore, he needed a certain amount of time for God to do some writing. Writing takes time. It took time for God to write upon those tablets. Similarly, in 2 Corinthians 3:3 Paul says, "Being manifested that you are a letter of Christ ministered by us, inscribed not with ink, but with the Spirit of the living God; not in tablets of stone, but in fleshy tablets of the heart." This is the New Testament writing — the writing of the Spirit on our hearts. In this context, precious time is being spent for this writing to take place. And while we are spending time under this writing upon our hearts, we are being transformed into the very image of our glorified Lord.

A private time

Without spending time with the Lord, there is no possibility for us to experience a solid transformation. And this time must be a private time with the Lord. The Lord makes this clear in Matthew 6. Beginning in verse 5 He says, "And when you pray, you shall not be as the hypocrites; for they love to pray standing in the synagogues and on the street corners that they may appear to men." The Lord points out here that the Pharisees were hypocrites because the motivation behind their kind of praying was to be seen of men. Then in verse 6 He says, "But you, when you pray, go into your private room." The Greek word for *private room* can also be translated as "inner chamber." The King James Version renders it "closet." All these translations—the private room, the inner chamber, and the closet—signify a personal, private time in a private place.

In verse 6 the Lord gives still further detailed instruction: after you go into your private room, *shut your door*. Shutting the door is a reinforcement of privacy, of aloneness with the Lord. And then He says, "pray to your Father who is in the secret place." The deep significance of having a private time with the Lord in a private place is that our transformation would be genuine and not something hypocritical. It should not be a performance. In our private time with the Lord, no one else is there. We open ourself to the Lord deeply, without any pretense, without any hypocrisy, without being motivated by any onlookers. There is no one else there saying anything or knowing anything. This means that our Christian life is taken out of the realm of man-pleasing and mere outward behavior and is brought into the reality of an intimate, personal relationship with the Lord. You are in a room with the Lord by yourself — four walls, a ceiling. What are you doing there? There must be reality in our contact with God.

In Matthew 6 we see how crucial it is to spend *private* time beholding the glory of the Lord. It takes this kind of time to be transformed. To simply spend two or three minutes reading some verses is not adequate for genuine transformation. It takes time for the writing of the Spirit on our being. Let me give a practical illustration. When we want to write on a tablet, the tablet has to "consent," so to speak, and spend some time in a fixed position. Then we can settle down and do some writing. However, if the tablet does not remain stationary, there is no way to write on it. The tablet has to consent by spending time there in one spot so that we can write. The tablet is an inanimate object. Our heart, on the other hand, is a moving object that needs to truly consent to remaining stationary before the Lord.

David's testimony in the Old Testament indicates that he had a heart that could remain fixed before the Lord. In Psalm 57:7 he said, "My heart is fixed, O God, my heart is fixed." Like David, we can also fix our heart. When our heart turns to the Lord the veil is taken away! A turned heart then becomes a fixed heart. As we spend time before Him, with our heart fixed and stationary, He can write His transforming life and nature into us.

To turn our heart means to stop our heart from all its preoccupations, from its endless stream of activity, and fix it on the Lord. Just as Moses brought the tablets of stone up to the mountain and spent time there in God's presence so that God could write on them, we too can turn our heart to the Lord and spend time being written upon by the Spirit of the living God.

When we turn our heart to the Lord, the writing Spirit (2 Cor. 3:3) is activated in us. This turning should not merely be a partial or shallow turn, but a deep turn that opens us up to the Lord and causes us to linger longer with the Lord for the Spirit to do His inner writing. It is this Spirit-writing that transforms us. As the Spirit writes upon us, we are transformed into the same image — the image of Christ Himself.

May the Lord give to us a spirit of wisdom and revelation to see God's eternal purpose of transforming us into the image of His Son. May we also realize that this purpose can only be fulfilled in us by our spending time beholding the Lord's glory. Let us, therefore, pay the price in our daily life to spend adequate time with Him. This is our greatest need.

3

How to Behold the Lord

"I never have seen a man or woman who spent fifteen or twenty minutes alone with God every day that didn't have the dew all the while. I have never known one to backslide, either. You never get more than one day's journey from Christ if you come to Him every morning. Shut the world out. Get closeted with God and you will learn His secrets. I like to get up at five o'clock in the morning and turn the key and be alone, and let God talk with me."

– D. L. Moody

The secret of spending time with the Lord is to learn how to behold the glory of the Lord. The apostle Paul says in 2 Corinthians 3:18, "And we all with unveiled face, beholding and reflecting as in a mirror the glory of the Lord, are being transformed into the same image from glory to glory, even as from the Lord Spirit." Our greatest need is this — to spend time with the Lord beholding His glory. God's purpose of reproducing the very image of Christ in us is fulfilled by beholding the Lord. Our being transformed and changed from within is realized by beholding the Lord. Everything we need will be supplied to us from the Lord Spirit by beholding Him.

If as a believer you are discouraged with yourself and frustrated in going on with the Lord, let me encourage you to lay aside everything and simply open to the Lord and say, "Lord, open my eyes and show me how to behold You. This is my greatest need." Indeed, the God-ordained way to proceed in the Christian life is to be a person restricted and reduced to beholding the glory of the Lord. Therefore, we need to consider some practical points on *how* to behold the glory of the Lord. These points are like handles to take hold of in order to experientially behold Him. If we take hold of these handles it can spiritually revolutionize our entire being.

Take the initiative

The first handle is to take the initiative. We have seen in chapter 1 that the nature of transformation is passive. It is a process that happens to us. The Lord Spirit changes us; we do not change ourselves. Paul makes this clear in 2 Corinthians 3:18 when he uses the passive voice "being transformed." The beholding in this verse, however, is not a passive matter. The unique thing about the Greek word for "beholding" here is that it is in the middle voice. In the Greek language a verb can have one of three different voices—active, middle, and passive. The active and passive voices are common to the English language, but the middle voice is not. Thus, we need to understand the middle voice and why Paul uses it for "beholding" in 2 Corinthians 3:18.

In Greek the active voice emphasizes the action, whereas the middle stresses the subject involved in the action. The writer's use of the middle voice shows his intention to emphasize that the subject is involved and participating in the action in a special way. This all indicates one thing in relation to beholding — it means we take the initiative. We as the subject are involved and participate in this spiritual action. We do not sit back and wait to be transformed by some sudden or mysterious power. No! We take the initiative to behold the glory of the Lord.

Strictly speaking, however, our initiative is not apart from God's divine operation within us. When we understand taking the initiative from God's point of view, we see that in reality it is our response to and cooperation with God's operation within our being. Let me say that if you are born-again, Christ is living in you and there is present within your being a divine working that is one-hundred percent bent on beholding the Lord. There is already something in you that matches this word on spending time to behold Him. You do not have to produce a desire in yourself in order to take the initiative. Check with your inner man. Look for the hidden desire within you, and see if there is not a corresponding burden and feeling about your spending time with the Lord.

If you are honest with your deepest sense, you will realize that day by day there is a still small voice within you speaking to you about spending time with the Lord — about enjoying and beholding Him. In fact, on the negative side, it feels like something nagging you. When you live neglecting your time with the Lord, there is something within you that spontaneously feels dissatisfied. You sense an incompleteness in your daily life even to the point of an inner protesting. On the positive side, however, there is a desire and a longing to be with the Lord in a definite way — to wait upon Him, behold Him, and enjoy Him. This desire and longing is God working in you.

Taking the initiative simply means to cooperate with what God has already put within you. The apostle Paul indicates this in Philippians 2:12-13: [12] "Work out your own salvation with fear and trembling; [13] for it is God who works in you both to will and to do for His good pleasure." The Greek word translated "work out" is similar to the word "beholding" in 2 Corinthians 3:18; that is, it is also in the middle voice. This means Paul intended to emphasize the need for the believers to take the initiative to be actively involved in and participate in the working out of their own salvation. However, the basis for taking this initiative is clearly defined by the following words: "For it is God who works in you." This means that the initiative we take is actually our going along with the operating God within us.

This is a crucial point in all our experiences of the Lord: God works and operates in us up to a certain extent; then we need to take the initiative to complete and finish what He is working in us. For example, we may live for years having desires to spend time with the Lord in a regular way. We may experience these desires to a greater or lesser degree, depending upon our spiritual situation. Nevertheless, we may not be aware of the fact that the very existence of these desires stirring within us *is* God operating in us.

God works in your will to incline you to spend time with Him. He operates to that extent. But He does not take us over and obliterate our faculties and human responsibility and force us to spend time with Him. He works in us to a point. Then it is up to us to take the initiative to follow through and cooperate with His worked-in inclinations and desires. In other words, God's part is to supply the desire and the inclination to be with Him. Our part is to find a private place to be with the Lord, set the alarm clock, rise up from our bed, wash our face, get our Bible, hymnal, and other spiritual books, and begin to wait upon the Lord—by reading, praying, singing, or just quietly being in His presence to enjoy Him and behold Him.

We need to realize that our desire to be with the Lord *is* God Himself. It is not just you. It is not just your desire. It is not merely your own thought that you should spend time with the Lord. It is God! God is in *your* desire! God is in *your* inclination! God is in *your* thought! Now you must work out what God has worked in. Just go along with that still small voice, that slight sensation that you should withdraw yourself to pray and spend time with Him. If you obey those small nudges, you are obeying God operating within you (Phil. 2:12-13).

Take the initiative every day. Go along with that little feeling within you. It may seem like it is merely you. But when you identify that feeling according to the Word of God, you discover that it is not you. It is God operating in you. Yet neither can you say that it is not you, because the desire is also *your* desire. Thus, we can say it is a *mingled* desire issuing from the divine life operating within our human life. The apostle Paul expressed this principle in 1 Corinthians 15:10

when he said, "But by the grace of God I am what I am, and His grace toward me was not in vain; but I labored more abundantly than they all, yet not I, but the grace of God which was with me." Paul admits that he labored, yet in reflecting on his own statement, he has to equally say, "yet not I, but the grace of God with me." By this statement we can see that taking the initiative ultimately means cooperating with God's operation.

So we can see that the first step in learning how to behold the glory of the Lord is that we take the initiative to do it. The Lord desires to do His work of transformation within us, but He is waiting for us to behold Him in order to accomplish it. Therefore, let us take the initiative with our whole heart to spend time with Him.

Make time to do it

The second handle in learning how to behold the glory of the Lord is simply to make time to do it. In Romans 12:2 the apostle Paul indicates that being "transformed by the renewing of your mind" is vitally related to not being conformed to this age. We have to admit that most of us have been conformed to this age in regard to how we spend our time. This age has so systematized our living and put us into its mold that it seems we can hardly squeeze in even five or ten minutes to spend time with the Lord. We are just too busy. Yet when something appeals to our natural life, we seem to find time to do that. For example, we may talk on the phone for thirty minutes to an hour, or we may somehow find time to read the newspaper or newsmagazine for forty-five minutes without thinking much about it. But when it comes to spending time with the Lord, we may go for days, weeks, months, or even years and make little effort to set apart even a small amount of time to be with Him. It is no wonder that we are not transformed into His image and that we have so many problems.

Making time to be with the Father was one of the most marked features of the Lord's life. As we read the Gospels, we see that He not only lived in the Father (John 14:10) and had continuous fellowship with the Father (John 8:29), but He also practiced regularly setting aside special time to be with the Father and pray.

The following verses reveal the Lord's own habits in spending time with the Father: "And rising very early in the morning, while it was still night, He went out and went away to a desolate place, and there He prayed" (Mark 1:35); "So He Himself often withdrew into the wilderness and prayed" (Luke 5:16); "Now it came to pass in those days that He went out to the mountain to pray, and continued all night in prayer to God" (Luke 6:12); [22] "And immediately He compelled the disciples to step into the boat and to go before Him to the other side, while He sent the crowds away. [23] And having sent the crowds away, He went up into the mountain privately to pray. And when evening came, He was there alone" (Matt. 14:22-23); "And it happened as He was alone praying, that His disciples joined Him, and He asked them, saying, Who do the crowds say that I am?" (Luke 9:18); [28] "And it came to pass, about eight days after these sayings, that He took Peter, John, and James and went up on the mountain to pray. [29] And it came about that as He prayed the appearance of His face became different, and His robe became white and glistening" (Luke 9:28-29); "And it came to pass, as He was praying in a certain place, when He ceased, that one of His disciples said to Him, Lord, teach us to pray, as John also taught his disciples" (Luke 11:1); [39] "And coming out, He went to the Mount of Olives, as He was accustomed, and His disciples also followed Him. . . . [41] And He was withdrawn from them about a stone's throw, and He knelt down and prayed" (Luke 22:39, 41).

By prayerfully considering all the above examples of the Lord's prayer life, we are deeply impressed that the Lord not only felt the need to spend time with the Father, but despite His busy schedule and ministry, He also made time to do it. Especially from Matthew 14:22-23 we can see how the Lord took control of His environment for the sake of spending time in prayer. He compelled His disciples to go to the other side of the sea, and He sent the crowds away — all in order to make time to be with the Father to pray in a private way.

In the same way, unless we take control of our daily schedules and environments for the sake of spending time with the Lord, our daily environments will take control of us! There is no easy, automatic way that we will fall into a habit of making time to be with the Lord. We must at times "compel" and "send away" in order to make time to be with Him.

Transformation depends upon our spending time with the Lord beholding His glory. Therefore, we must cooperate with those mingled desires by taking the initiative to make the time to do it. Every effort spent in this direction will be greatly rewarded. The Lord Himself promises a reward to those who exercise themselves to make time to be with Him. He says in Matthew 6:6, "But you, when you pray, go into your private room, and when you have shut your door, pray to your Father who is in the secret place, and your Father who sees in secret will reward you openly."

Position your heart

The third handle that we can lay hold of in learning how to behold the glory of the Lord is to position our heart. Once we take the initiative to cooperate with the Lord and actually make time to be with Him, we then discover what kind of person we are. We find out what the real condition of our heart is — how distracted we are, how prone we are to be filled with wandering thoughts, even while we are spending time with the Lord. We often fall into morbid introspection about our sinful condition. The devil injects his suggestive thoughts. And on top of all this, our body is weak and we find ourselves falling asleep or dulled and dazed. So after we win the battle over making the time to be with the Lord, we then find out that during our time with Him there is another battle to be won. What shall we do in light of all this?

In facing the battle during our time with the Lord, we need to position our heart by turning it to the Lord. Paul says in 2 Corinthians 3:16, "But whenever it [the heart] turns to the Lord, the veil is taken away." Then he continues in verse 18, "But we all, with unveiled face, beholding and reflecting as in a mirror the glory of the Lord . . ." These verses show us that in order to behold the Lord with an unveiled face we need a *turned* heart. A turned heart is one that is positioned toward the Lord. In other words, our heart has been turned in another direction — away from the Lord — and we need to turn it toward the Lord.

Our heart may be distracted by many things, but our one and only need is to turn it toward the Lord. Our tendency is to have our heart turned toward our problems or turned toward our defeated condition or turned toward what we see in ourselves that is still not subdued by the Lord. But the most important thing in spending time with the Lord is to get our eyes off ourselves and onto Him. Regardless of how we feel or what we see in ourselves, we still need to keep our heart focused on the Lord.

Hebrews 2:8-9 tells us clearly what our focus should be: [8] "You have put all things in subjection under His feet. For in that He put all in subjection under Him, He left nothing that is not put under Him. But now we do not yet see all things subjected to Him, [9] *but we see Jesus . . .*" There are two things to take note of in these verses. First, the fact that "we do not yet see all things put under Him"; and second, "but we see Jesus." These two things are going on at the same time. That means we may see many things in us that are not yet subjected to Him — things that are not under His feet, under His ruling. But even in such an unfinished state, we still see Jesus! Our heart can be positioned and focused on Christ despite the existence of the unsubjected things. So do not be distracted or discouraged by what you see in yourself. Keep your eyes upon Jesus and trust *Him* to subdue every unruly thing.

Position your heart by using your spirit and say, "Lord, with my spirit and with the eyes of my heart I want to behold You. Lord, I don't care for all the distractions and the things that are not yet subjected under Your feet. Lord, I just care for You. Show me Yourself. Let me see Your glory." It is not by our striving or human effort that we get transformed into the image of Christ, but by positioning our heart before Him with the deliberate exercise of our spirit. If we will daily take the initiative, make time to do it, and position our hearts, we will keep ourselves in the place where God Himself can change us.

Let the glory of His person and work pass before you

When Moses was on the mountain in Exodus 33:18-19, he said to the Lord, "Please, show me Your glory." The Lord's reply to this request was simply, "I will make all My goodness pass before you, and I will proclaim the name of the LORD before you." The Lord further responded to Moses in verse 22 by saying, "So it shall be, while My glory passes by, that I will put you in the cleft of the rock, and will cover you with My hand while I pass by." Following this speaking, the same morning that Moses presented himself to the Lord to see His glory, Exodus 34:5-7 says, [5] "Then the LORD descended in the cloud and stood with him there, and proclaimed the name of the LORD. [6] And the LORD passed before him and proclaimed, 'The LORD, the LORD God, merciful and gracious, longsuffering, and abounding in goodness and truth, [7] keeping mercy for thousands, forgiving iniquity and transgression and sin.' "

The Lord's answer to Moses' request, "Please, show me Your glory," consisted of a wonderful heavenly scenery passing before him. Four times in these accounts the Lord emphasized the matter of Moses seeing something pass before him: "I will make all My goodness *pass* before you," "My glory *passes* by," "I *pass* by," and "the LORD *passed* before him and proclaimed." From these verses we can see that to behold the Lord's glory means to see the scenery of His Person and His work pass before us. It was his beholding of this scenery that transformed Moses so that "the skin of his face shone" (Exo. 34:30).

For Moses to behold the scenery of God's glory passing by, the Lord told him that He would put him in the cleft of the rock and cover him with His hand (Exo. 33:22). In typology, being in the cleft of the rock signifies being hidden in the crucified Christ, who died for us on the cross and shed His precious blood so that we can approach God directly and behold His glory. Thus, because of Christ's blood, because of His finished work, because of that once-and-for-all sacrifice, because He entered into the Holiest of All and made a way for us to be there and live there — now we can fully enjoy the glory of the Lord by letting this redemptive scenery pass before our spiritual eyes.

Only the blood of Jesus ushers us into the glory. Growth as a Christian does not get us into the glory. Being a believer for twenty-five or fifty years does not merit our getting into the glory. Only one thing qualifies us to enjoy the glory of the Lord — the precious blood of the Lamb. That is all — just the blood. We can declare, "I'm forgiven, I'm washed, I'm cleansed, and now I'm qualified to behold the Lord face to face." Paul describes this privilege in 2 Corinthians 4:6 as our having "the knowledge of the glory of God in the face of Jesus Christ."

When Moses was on the mountain with God, he was not doing anything, he was not analyzing his own situation, he was not looking at himself. He was simply there watching the scenery, watching everything pass by him. Moses just presented himself and God passed by proclaiming His name, His goodness, His mercy, and His forgiveness. It was after seeing all of this that Moses came down from the mountain shining.

In the same way, in 2 Corinthians 3:18 Paul says, "But we all, with unveiled face, beholding . . . the glory of the Lord." To behold this glory we need to exercise ourselves to let the glory of Christ's Person and work pass before us. Paul practiced this principle of beholding in his preaching of the gospel. Thus, he could write to the Galatians about the Lord Jesus being openly portrayed crucified before their eyes (Gal. 3:1). By seeing such a gospel scenery they came under "the hearing of faith" and received the Spirit (Gal. 3:2). In other words, they received the Spirit by letting the crucified Christ pass before them by means of hearing the gospel. They beheld His Person and work and were infused with the Holy Spirit.

There are many other verses in the New Testament that talk about beholding the Lord, such as beholding the "glory as of the only Begotten from the Father" in John 1:14, seeing Jesus in Hebrews 2:9, seeing the ascended Son of Man in John 6:62, beholding His glory in John 17:24, and looking away unto Jesus in Hebrews 12:2. These kinds of verses stress the importance of daily allowing the Lord's entire redemptive process to pass before us, including His incarnation, human living, crucifixion, resurrection, ascension, and enthronement.

We also need to behold all that the Lord's wonderful Person is, including all His attributes. What transforms us is seeing His mercy, His kindness, His goodness, His righteousness, His holiness, and His worthiness. All that Jesus is and all that He has passed through in His redemptive process needs to become our daily scenery. To be transformed, we simply need to spend time with the Lord and let this scenery pass before us. Every day, even every hour, we can behold the glory of the Lord.

With the eyes of our heart and with our spirit, we can cultivate our beholding of the Lord through songs, the Word, and prayer. These are the ways to enjoy and behold the glory of the Lord passing before our spiritual vision. We need to nurture this kind of spiritual exercise. We have our home life, our family life, our social life, our school life, and our work life. We meet people and talk to people. We are occupied daily with many things. Although we have this kind of life outwardly, we also need to preserve a secret life in a private room with the door shut, spending time with the Lord (Matt. 6:6). Here there is no one else but ourself and the Lord. Here we can behold His glory by praying, by singing, and by reading the Word.

Spending time with the Lord is revolutionary in our experience. We may think we need to grit our teeth a little more and say, "Lord, this time I'm going to make it through as a victorious believer." This kind of resolution, no matter how sincere, is nothing but our own energy and effort, and is bound to fail. Actually, we only need one thing — time with the Lord in a private place.

So take the initiative and reschedule your life to go along with that still small voice prodding you to spend time with the Lord. And then just position your heart before the glory of the Lord. Do not worry about what is not yet under His feet (Heb. 2:8-9). Just let the Lord's Person and work pass by. You can behold Him because you are in the cleft of the rock — in the crucified One. You are under the precious blood. So you and I can enjoy all that the Lord is. Then we will be transformed into the same image from glory to glory.

This is how beholding the glory of the Lord transforms us into the same image. It is very simple. It is just a matter of doing it — taking the initiative, taking time, finding a private place, positioning our heart, and then just exposing ourself to the transforming element of the Lord's glory passing before our eyes. We see Jesus. Hallelujah!

Find a hymnal and sing, making melody in your heart to the Lord. Take the verses of the Bible and pray with them and over them. Then at other times just open yourself to the Lord and tell Him you love Him. Get acquainted with the blood of the Lamb in the book of Revelation and how all the redeemed are singing about it in the heavens (Rev. 5:9-14; 7:9-14; 12:10-11; 14:2-4). Join in with the heavens and sing about His precious blood. Speak to the Lord about His wonderful Person and work. Your beholding and enjoying Him in this kind of way will become your transformation.

Oh, may the Lord give us such a personal, secret, intimate life with Him. Then we will be solid, we will grow, the devil will be defeated, we will discover that the Lord will take us up into His own intercessory life to carry out His purpose and His plan. All of this issues from our spending time daily with the Lord and letting the glory of His Person and work pass before us.

4

The Life Christ Lives in Us

"Receiving Christ and through Him united to God, there comes to us the stupendous blessing expressed in these words 'that the love wherewith Thou hast loved Him may be in them.' We become the objects of the very same love which the Father has for His Son. We are recognized as part of Him even as the bride is taken into her husband's family and loved even as her husband. This is, indeed, the mystery of mysteries: that we are permitted to share the intimate and exclusive affection of the eternal Father toward His only begotten Son. He loves us now, not for ourselves, nor in proportion to our personal claims upon His affection, but precisely as He loves Jesus Christ, with infinite complacency and unlimited measure."

– A. B. Simpson

The Lord's life in the Gospels and in us

By observing the Lord's life on the earth, we can become more familiar with the Lord's life within us. The one unique life that is described in the four Gospels is *the very same life* that is now living in us. Thus, by studying the Lord's life in the Gospels, we are not merely considering something objective or outside of us, but something that is also subjective in our spirit. His life lived out in the Gospels is what is now being reproduced in us by His indwelling.

As Christians we can have the assurance that the same Christ who was once outside of us is the Christ who is now inside of us. Furthermore, the *way* Christ lived on the earth is precisely the same way He is living in us. We must see that the kind of life He lived in the flesh is not something different from the life He now lives in us. This is a basic biblical principle—learning how to apply the Lord's life in the flesh to our own experience of Him in the spirit.

The apostle Paul spoke according to this principle in Ephesians 4:20-21 when he said to the believers, [20] "But you have not so learned Christ, [21] if indeed you have heard Him and have been taught in Him, as the truth is in Jesus." To "learn Christ" is to learn Him by His example in the four Gospels; and "the truth in Jesus" means that Jesus lived a life of truth, or reality, by always doing things *in* the Father, *with* the Father, and *for* the Father. This was the truth in Jesus demonstrated and recorded in the Gospels.

Now as believers having Christ as our life and being taught in the realm of our spirit union with Him (1 Cor. 6:17), we come to learn that the *same* relationship He had with the Father in the flesh is the same kind of experience being repeated in us in the spirit. We "have heard Him and have been taught in Him." Thus, to adequately learn the indwelling Christ in our experience, we need two things: we need to study the Lord's example in the Gospels and to watch how that same life is being worked out in our union with Him in the details of our daily life.

Another passage that reveals this same principle is Philippians chapter 2. In verse 5 Paul says, "Let this mind be in you which was also in Christ Jesus." Following this statement Paul continues to describe the Lord's attitude of humility in His incarnation and human living, setting it forth as an example of what believers are to expect God to work in them. In other words, the mind and disposition that was "in Christ Jesus" in the four Gospels is the same mind and disposition that is being wrought into us as a result of the indwelling Christ.

By applying this principle to our spending time with the Lord, we observe one of the most striking features of the Lord's life recorded in the Gospels—how He spent time with the Father. The following passages reveal this: Mark 1:35; Luke 5:16; 6:12; 9:18, 28-29; 11:1; 22:39, 41; and Matthew 14:22-23. In the midst of His ministry, He was often slipping away to spend time alone with the Father to pray. This aspect of the Lord's earthly life teaches us that the same Christ now living within us still needs time for fellowship and prayer with the Father. If we follow the Lord in His prayer life in the Gospels, we discover many helpful points regarding how the Lord spent time with the Father. What was true of Him then is still true of Him now as He continues to live His life in us. Thus, we can learn Christ in us and how to spend time with Him by considering how He spent time with the Father.

The Lord's love relationship with the Father

In considering the Lord's prayer life, the first question we must look into is, what motivated Him to spend so much time with the Father? The answer is simply—love. Indeed, the outstanding feature that characterized the Lord's earthly life was His love relationship with the Father. This can be seen in John 1:18: "No one has seen God at any time; the only begotten Son, who is *in* the bosom of the Father, He has declared Him." The preposition "in" in this verse is better translated "into" (Gk. εἰς). It should read, "the only begotten Son, who is *into* the bosom of the Father." There is a difference between "in" and "into." "In" implies a stationary position, whereas "into" implies motion and movement into something. Thus, the preposition "into" in John 1:18 describes the motion and movement within the intimate love relationship the Son had with the Father.

Frederick L. Godet, in his classic commentary on the Gospel of John, makes the following comment on this love relationship: "This present participle *who is* (ὁ ὤν) refers to the permanent relation of the Son to the Father through all the stages of His divine, human, and divine-human existence. He ever presses anew with an equal intimacy into the bosom of the Father, who reveals Himself to Him in a manner suitable to His position and His work at every moment. The form εἰς κόλπον [*into* the bosom], instead of ἐν κόλπῳ [*in* the bosom] (the preposition of motion, instead of that of rest), expresses precisely this active and living relation. The bosom of the Father is not a place, but a life; one *is there* only in virtue of a continual moral act." Thus, to say the Lord was "into the bosom of the Father" is a very descriptive and intimate way of revealing the Lord's love relationship with the Father.

The secret to the Lord's life of expressing the Father, of His being so one with the Father, and of His always pleasing the Father was His love-life *into* the bosom of the Father. The Lord's human life consisted of His habit of continually spending time pressing anew into the bosom of the Father and allowing the Father's love to saturate Him. The Lord said in John 15:9-10, [9] "As the Father loved Me, I also have loved you; abide in My love. [10] If you keep My commandments, you will abide in My love, just as I have kept My Father's commandments and abide in His love." This was the key to the Lord's daily life. He knew how to spend time with the Father, abiding in His love.

Now the Lord's life indwelling us is exactly the same as it was in the Gospels. It is still a love-life pressing ever anew into the bosom of the Father. That is why the Lord commands all His believers to abide in His love. This is our greatest need in spending time with the Lord — just to abide in His love. However, with so many of us, the problem is that we abide in our present condition, we abide in our failures, we abide in our past record, we abide in our concepts, and we abide in our anxieties about the future. In other words, we abide in everything but His love. We know all about ourselves and can dissect our problems accurately, but we know very little about spending time with the Lord, basking in the sunshine of His love.

Let me ask, how is your love relationship with the Lord? Is He sweet? (S. of S. 5:16). Is He intimate? (S. of S. 1:2-4). Do you enjoy Him as the One who loves you and shed His blood for you? (Rev. 1:5). If you do not enjoy the Lord in this way, then you need to reevaluate your whole Christian life. Are you trying to live an overcoming life in your own strength? Have you fallen into the Galatian error of beginning by the Spirit but then endeavoring to be perfected by the flesh? (Gal. 3:3). Are you struggling to improve your behavior? Are you even serving and working for the Lord but still lacking a sweet and intimate love relationship with Him? Perhaps your entire Christian life is one defeat after another simply because you have neglected to spend time fellowshipping with Him and abiding in His love.

Cultivating a love relationship with the Lord

We must be clear concerning this matter. It takes time to cultivate a love relationship with the Lord. This was demonstrated by the Lord's own earthly life. He repeatedly spent time with the Father, enjoying the Father's love (Luke 5:16). In Mark 14:36 we find the Lord in the garden of Gethsemane, where it was His habit to go and be with the Father (Luke 22:39). Here He was once again pressing anew into the bosom of the Father while facing the critical hour of crucifixion. Mark records in verse 36 that He was saying repeatedly, "Abba, Father." This means that even when He became obedient unto death, the death of the cross, He was doing it by enjoying the Father's love. To say "Abba" is to call upon the Father in the most sweet and intimate way.

Now we must see that this same "Abba, Father" love-life that the Lord demonstrated in the garden has been sent into our hearts in Galatians 4:6. Here Paul declares, "And because you are sons, God has sent forth the Spirit of His Son into our hearts, crying, Abba, Father!" What a joy! What a hope! The very prayer life of God's Son is in our hearts. The intimate love-life between the Father and the Son has been put into us. We have it! It is not a matter of trying to find it or longing to possess it. We already have the Triune God's love-life within us. And just by virtue of our being a born-again Christian, we are entitled to merge in our hearts with the love flowing between the Father and the Son in the fellowship of the Holy Spirit (2 Cor. 13:14).

Now the Lord's love-life with the Father simply needs to be cultivated and released in us. That life is in us twenty-four hours a day — the same life that cried "Abba, Father," the same life that withdrew so many times into the wilderness to pray, the same life that wanted to be with the Father alone — that life is in us. And this life in us needs time. The same life that took time to pray in the Gospels still needs time to pray in us. The Spirit of His Son is located within our hearts, waiting for us to join in and cry "Abba, Father" (cf. Gal. 4:6 and Rom. 8:15-16). What an indescribable enjoyment—that we could merge with the Son's life which is ever pressing anew with equal intimacy into the bosom of the Father.

Spending time with the Lord in this way will supply us, deliver us, save us, and transform us. We do not need human effort, religion, or outward improvement of behavior. We do not need to adjust ourselves with our natural energy. We just need time to be with the Lord to allow ourselves to abide in His love.

The Lord further described our participation in this love-life of the Triune God in John 17:26 by saying to the Father,

"And I have declared to them Your name, and will declare it, that the love with which You loved Me may be in them, and I in them." This means exactly what it says: the very same love that Jesus enjoyed from the Father is in us, not imitated by us or worked up by us. We experience the Triune God's love-life dwelling in us by allowing this love-life to pass through our being from our spirit (Rom. 8:15) into our heart (Gal. 4:6). In light of this, who would be so foolish as to neglect spending time with the Lord enjoying this flow of liquid love!

Who can fathom the intensity of the Father's love and delight in His beloved Son? Step out of yourself for a moment. Do not consider your condition. Stop your struggle for victory. Cease from all your preoccupations. Just stop and consider one thing—the Father's love to the Son! The Father declared from the heavens at Jesus' baptism, "This is My beloved Son, in whom I am well pleased" (Matt. 3:17). The Son is the Father's delight! Not you, not me, not our condition, but the Son! The flow of the Father's love is all channeled to the Son.

Now listen to John 17:26 once more: "That the love with which You loved Me MAY BE IN THEM, AND I IN THEM." What you and I need is not to find out how to solve our problems, but rather to place ourselves before the Lord and to simply give Him some time for His love-life to pass through us. The flow of the divine love conveyed to us by the Spirit (John 7:37-39) not only solves our problems, but brings us everything we need. The love-life of the Triune God Himself is our portion and enjoyment. We just need to spend time cultivating it.

Putting Himself aside

In observing how the Lord spent time with the Father we also need to see how He put Himself aside. Luke 3:21 says, "Now when all the people were baptized, it came to pass that Jesus also was baptized; and while He prayed, the heaven was opened." Here we can see the Lord's prayer life in a unique way — in its relationship to the meaning of baptism. Baptism means to put oneself aside, to bury oneself (cf. Rom. 6:3-6). Thus, while He was putting Himself aside in the death waters of baptism, He was praying. This implies that in spending time with the Father to pray on this occasion, He was putting Himself aside. All that He was as a man in the flesh (John 1:14; Rom. 8:3), He put aside in baptism by prayer. Following this act, Luke 3:22 says, "And the Holy Spirit descended in bodily form like a dove upon Him, and a voice came from heaven which said, You are My beloved Son; in You I am well pleased." In other words, putting Himself aside with prayer made a way for the Spirit to come in with God's speaking.

The same principle must apply to our experience of the Lord. In spending time with Him we must put ourselves aside. We have to say, "Lord, I put myself aside — all my distractions, all my fears, all my anxieties, all my condemnation, all my preoccupation with myself. Lord, I come to You to put myself aside." This is the practical significance of baptism and praying. And in spending time with the Lord, this is an important factor. We have to learn to put aside the intruding thoughts that pop into our mind, such as," I don't know how to spend time with the Lord. I've failed in the past. I don't think this is going to work for me." These kinds of thoughts must be put aside. Every distracting thought that enters into our mind must be put aside.

During the initial period of spending time with the Lord, it is good to take a little time to just put yourself aside in every dimension — put aside your feelings of failure, put aside your natural life, put aside your environment, put aside your present dealings, put aside what *you* think the Lord is speaking to you. Many times we imagine the Lord is saying something and doing something, yet it may not be Him at all. It may be our own thought.

It is much better to remain in the principle of baptism. It is much better to bury everything, that is, to put aside our natural life, our religious life, and even our spiritual life. Just bury it! Absolutely put yourself aside. Tell Him, "Lord, I really don't know You that well. I know the doctrines of Christianity, I know many things about You, and I know what I'm supposed to be. But Lord, I want to get to know *You.* So, Lord, I just put myself aside."

In Colossians chapter 2, the apostle Paul applied the principle of baptism to the believers at the very time they were being distracted by so many religious ordinances. The Colossians had been influenced by certain heretical teachings that caused them to focus on themselves rather than putting themselves aside. Such dogmatic slogans as "Do not touch, do not taste, do not handle" (Col. 2:21) all tended to turn the believers in on themselves. They were caught up in "self-imposed religion, false humility, and neglect of the body" (Col. 2:23). They were all entangled in the knots of their own self-effort. Though they were spending time seeking the Lord, they were doing it from the source of themselves. Instead of causing the self to be put aside, the heretical teachings caused them to rely and depend upon the self.

In this distracted situation, Paul brings them back to the meaning of their baptism by saying, [11] "In Him you were also circumcised with the circumcision made without hands, by putting off the body of the sins of the flesh, by the circumcision of Christ, [12] buried with Him in baptism" (Col. 2:11-12). In essence Paul was saying, "You have been terminated! You have been put aside!" So then he says, [1] "Seek those things which are above, where Christ is, sitting at the right hand of God. [2] Set your mind on things above, not on things on the earth" (Col. 3:1-2). In other words, the proper way to spend time with the Lord, seeking Him, is to do so as a terminated person. This means we put ourselves aside in order to fully enjoy our union with the love-life of the Triune God. Paul puts it plainly: "For you died, and your life is hidden with Christ in God" (Col. 3:3).

To put ourselves aside is to go along with the real significance of our baptism — that is, we were terminated! The goal of this termination has in view that we would be a person who is *reduced* to the love-life of the Triune God. Indeed, God's eternal counsel concerning us is that we would share in the continuous flow of love between the Father and the Son (Eph. 1:4-5). Thus, we must put ourselves aside in order to cultivate this love that flows in the Triune God and that has reached out to take us up into Himself, making us organically the Body of Christ (Eph. 5:25, 28-30).

From eternity past to eternity future God's love is over us and with us. In fact, nothing can separate us from the love of God which is in Christ Jesus our Lord. No principalities, powers, death, life — whatever realm — nothing can separate us. We are more than conquerors, not through our condition, not through our potential, but through Him who loved us. However, if we do not spend time with the Lord and put ourselves aside, we may be cheated from the daily enjoyment of this mighty flowing love.

Paul lived in the enjoyment of this love, and that love was the realm whereby Christ lived in him. In Galatians 2:20 he said, "I have been crucified with Christ." That means I am put out of the way, I am terminated. "It is no longer I." I have been put aside. Now it is Christ who lives in me. Then Paul adds, "and the life which I now live in the flesh," that is, in the environment of my flesh — the strivings of my flesh, the anxieties of my flesh, the depression of my flesh, all the things of my flesh — the life I now live in this environment, I will tell you how I live: "I live by faith, the faith of the Son of God, who loved me and gave Himself for me." Paul does not say, "loved us," but "loved me." That was how personal and intimate the Lord's love was to Paul, and this was what motivated him to enjoy this living Person.

So in spending time with the Lord to cultivate a love relationship with Him, we must put ourself aside to hear God's voice speaking about His Son: "In Him I am well pleased." Just forget about yourself. Let the Lord speak that word to you, "I delight in Him." And then tell Him, "Lord,

You are the Father's delight. I treasure this time that I could spend in prayer enjoying You, the One who is the Father's delight." It is in this loving interchange in our spirit between us and the Lord, with the eyes of our heart gazing upon Him, that we are spontaneously being transformed.

Observing the Lord's life and how He spent time with the Father, we have first seen His love relationship with the Father, and second how He put Himself aside. So regardless of your condition or how you feel when you spend time with the Lord, every condition and every feeling is just good for one thing — to be put aside. It is just good to put it aside. Stay in the reality of your baptism. That is all. And pray. Turn away from all the distractions and merge with the love-life of the Triune God. This is what we need. This is what we desperately need — we just need to spend time enjoying God.

5

Spending Time with the Lord in the Word

"My mind being now more open and enlarged, I began to read the Holy Scriptures upon my knees, laying aside all other books, and praying over, if possible, every line and word. This proved meat indeed and drink indeed to my soul. I daily received fresh life, light, and power from above. I got more true knowledge from reading the Book of God in one month than I could ever have acquired from all the writings of men. In one word, I found it profitable for reproof, for correction, for instruction in righteousness, every way sufficient to make the man of God perfect, thoroughly furnished unto every good word and work."

– George Whitefield

Feeding upon the Word

To learn how to spend time with the Lord in a profitable way, we need to consider how the Lord Himself spent time with the Father. By doing this we will discover that the same principles that governed His earthly life also govern His life now indwelling us. How He lived on the earth is how He now lives in us (Heb. 13:8).

We have seen that one of the secrets of the Lord's spending time with the Father was how He cultivated His love relationship with the Father (John 1:18; 15:9-10). We have also seen that another secret of His spending time with the Father was how He practiced putting Himself aside as He prayed (Luke 3:21). Now we must observe a third crucial secret out of the Lord's life that should also govern our spending time with the Lord. This was the Lord's practice and habit of feeding upon the Word.

In Matthew 4:4 the Lord declared to the devil, "It is written, man shall not live by bread alone, but by every word that proceeds from the mouth of God." These words quoted by the Lord from Deuteronomy 8:3 not only reveal how He handled the devil's attacks, but they also show us the secret of His inner life. It is clear that the strength of the Lord's inner life was maintained by His regular feeding upon the Word. He was not living by bread alone, but by every word proceeding out through the mouth of God. So the Word is likened here to something that nourishes — bread.

If the Lord felt the need to spend time with the Father, feeding upon the Word, how much more do we need this kind of practice. The Lord Jesus was intrinsically the living Word (Gk. λόγος), yet He took time to feed on the written Word; and He could testify to the devil that this was the way He was living. He was living on every word proceeding out through the mouth of God.

Now we must see that our inner life is constituted with the same inner life that was in Christ Jesus. The apostle Paul makes this clear in 1 Corinthians 6:17: "He who is joined to the Lord is one spirit with Him." Our human spirit, which has been regenerated through the new birth, is now mingled with the Lord Himself who is the Spirit (2 Cor. 3:17; 1 Cor. 15:45). Thus, what was true of the Lord's life in the flesh is still true of His life in resurrection as the life-giving Spirit dwelling in our spirit (2 Tim. 4:22). Now we must come to know in our experience how our inner man needs and requires regular times to feed upon the Word (1 Pet. 2:2-3). This was one of the Lord's secrets in maintaining His supply to live out the Father's life, and it must become our secret as well (John 6:57).

When the Lord says, "every word that *proceeds* out," He uses a present-tense participle. He does not use the past tense. He does not say, "Man shall live on every word that *proceeded* out of the mouth of God centuries ago when the Bible was written by Moses and all the other Old Testament writers." No, He says, "every word that is *presently proceeding* out of the mouth of God." In other words, the Lord's view of the Word was that it was the present speaking of God. When we come to the Bible we should come in the same way: "Lord, this Word was not only originally breathed out by You, but it is still breathing You."

The nature of this Bible is spirit and life. In John 6:63 the Lord said, "The words that I speak to you, they are spirit and they are life." This means that the inner content of every verse, every word, is spirit and life. It is nourishing and it will supply you. It will change your insides. Simply open up and pray and use your praying spirit with the Word. Do not just think about the words, but pray, "Lord, thank You for Your Word. Thank

You for such a verse as, 'Man shall not live by bread alone, but by every word that proceeds from the mouth of God.' "

To take the Word in a spiritual way for supply is in contrast to just reading it as you would read *Reader's Digest.* When you come to the Word you are not just exercising your mind — not just reading for mere information — but stopping, opening up to God with the realization, "This is Your breathing to me right now, Lord." Such an opening means this Word is intended to supply me with God Himself. It is to nourish me for today. It is like opening your mouth up to eat your meal, and the food gives you energy and fuel to supply your physical body. Now we can echo our Lord, "Lord, thank You, I'm not living by bread alone, but by every word proceeding out of Your mouth. Thank You, Lord, for Your precious Word that proceeds out." Begin to talk to the Lord with the words of the Bible.

A personal testimony

As a believer, some years ago I began to learn this secret of feeding on the Word. After being a Christian for about nine years, I came to a point where I felt dry, discouraged, and defeated. I had tried to overcome my failing self in many areas, but found that I lacked the necessary strength. This went on for several weeks, and then somehow it occurred to me that I should begin reading my Bible three times a day in a regular way. So I began reading the Old Testament in the morning, Psalms and Proverbs at noon, and the New Testament in the evening. It was amazing to see what happened to me within one week. I discovered that the Word of God was food! At that time the Lord impressed me with Jeremiah 15:16, "Thy words were found, and I did eat them, and thy word was unto me the joy and rejoicing of mine heart: for I am called by thy name, O Lord God of hosts." This verse became my experience and testimony.

Formerly, my time with the Lord in the Word had been mainly an exercise of my eyes and my mind. But when I discovered that the nature of God's Word was food, I began to read the Word with a praying spirit. The Bible became a new book in my hands — it became a book of enjoyment, a book from which I could feed upon the living God. I found myself reading and praying simultaneously and then taking up a verse or a phrase and beginning to fellowship with the Lord with the very words of Scripture. I found I did not have to strive to find what to pray. The Word of God itself became the content of my prayer.

While doing this I found a mysterious yet real supply spontaneously infusing my inner man. No longer was I merely looking at black and white letters on a page or trying to mentally understand things, which had often left me spiritually deadened. For the first time in my Christian life, I began to enjoy God Himself in the pages of the Bible.

Eating three square meals a day by feeding upon the Word taught me experientially that my inner man requires food just as my physical body does. The reason for my defeated Christian life, I discovered, was simply lack of nourishment. Even though I had been studying the Bible for seven years in Bible college and seminary, it had become to me a book of theology, sermons, and outlines, rather than a book of enjoyment and supply. I realized that the mere knowledge of the Bible could not change me. It was only when the Bible was translated into food by praying with my spirit over the verses that it turned into enjoyment rather than mere thought. I began to experience a living supply that automatically filled me with God. I realized then as I do today, many years later, that one of the secrets of spending time with the Lord is to feed upon the Word.

Our view of the Bible

What does it mean to feed upon the Word? First, we must see that to the Lord it meant having a living and fresh relationship with the written Scriptures. For example, in Matthew 4:4 when the Lord said, "It is written," He used the perfect tense in Greek (γέγραπται), which can be literally translated, "It stands written." He did not say, "It was written," as though the Word was something merely recorded in the past without any present reality. The force of the perfect tense, "It stands written," indicates that the Lord's attitude toward the Word was that it was God's *present* speaking — living and fresh, not dead and old.

As we saw earlier, the written Scriptures were identified by the Lord as being the very word that "proceeds out through the mouth of God." In saying "proceeds," the Lord again used a tense that revealed His attitude toward the written Scriptures. "Proceeds" is a present participle (ἐκπορευομένῳ), which denotes that "every word" was presently proceeding out through the mouth of God. He did not use the past tense "proceeded," as though He was articulating a theory on the inspiration of Scripture. Instead, He used the present tense "proceeds" to reveal that the written Scriptures are living and fresh, even proceeding "out through the mouth of God." This proceeding word, according to the Lord's view, is good for man not only to study and read, but to feed upon as bread and to live by. This was the Lord's realization concerning the Scriptures. Consequently, in His experience His relationship to them was characterized by feeding upon the Word to be nourished and strengthened.

In the same way, our view of the Bible will determine how we handle it and come to it. If our view is that the Bible is a book of knowledge and doctrines, then the time we spend with it will be characterized by study and research with no life (John 5:38-40). However, if our realization of the Bible is that it is living and fresh, proceeding out through God's mouth for us to be nourished, then the time we spend with it will be characterized by enjoyment and feeding with much life supply (Job 23:12; Psa. 119:103; Heb. 6:5).

The nature of the Bible

Our view of the Bible should be based on our understanding of the nature of the Bible. The nature of the Bible is clearly defined in 2 Timothy 3:16: "All Scripture is *God-breathed,* and is profitable for doctrine, for reproof, for correction, for instruction in righteousness." Most English versions use the words "given by inspiration of God" or "inspired of God" when translating the compound Greek word *theopneustos* (θεόπνευστος). However, it is best rendered literally "God-breathed." Second Timothy 3:16 is the only occurrence of this word in the New Testament. It is also used by some ancient Greek writers and is variously understood either in a passive sense or an active sense.

When we understand the word *theopneustos* passively, it is translated "All Scripture is God-breathed" and emphasizes the fact that when the Scriptures were originally given, they were the breath of God as the biblical writers penned them. However, when we understand *theopneustos* actively, it is translated "All Scripture is God breathing" and emphasizes the fact that the *written* Scriptures are presently God's breath to us. Both the passive and active senses are supported by other passages, and thus both are true. The pietistic Bible teacher John Albert Bengel expressed it well in his comments on 2 Timothy 3:16: "It was divinely inspired, not merely while it was written, God breathing through the writers, but also while it is being read, God breathing through the Scripture, and the Scripture breathing Him."

The Scriptures were "God-breathed" when they were written, and they are presently "God breathing" while they are being read and poured over with prayer. Today when we come to the Word and open our hearts to the Lord, we touch the nature of the Scriptures as God's breath and are supplied to live by that Word. Paul speaks of this kind of relationship with the Word in Colossians 3:16 when he says, "Let the word of Christ dwell in you richly in all wisdom, teaching and admonishing one another in psalms and hymns and spiritual songs, singing with grace in your hearts to the Lord." In this verse we see that our relationship with the Lord is very much related to our relationship with the Word in a way of praying and singing. The richness of our contact with Christ is in proportion to our contact with *the Word* of Christ. When we allow the Word of Christ to indwell us richly, we become partakers of the divine nature through the Word (2 Pet. 1:4). By handling the Word with a praying spirit, we discover that it becomes God's breath to us.

Just reflect a little bit on this statement, "All Scripture is God-breathed." This means that the nature of Scripture is different from that of all other writings. Although the Scriptures were written by men, these men were moved and carried along by the Holy Spirit. Second Peter 1:20-21 says, [20] "Knowing this first, that no prophecy of Scripture is of any private interpretation, [21] for prophecy never came by the will of man, but holy men of God spoke as they were moved by the Holy Spirit." Thus, when the New Testament writers quote the Old Testament writers, they do it in a way that emphasizes the nature of the Scriptures. For example, Acts 1:16 records Peter as saying, "This Scripture had to be fulfilled, which the Holy Spirit spoke before by the mouth of David." And Mark 12:36 says, "David himself said by the Holy Spirit." In other words, whatever David said was equally the Holy Spirit's speaking. Thus, the nature of all Scripture is God's very Spirit-breath.

In Ephesians 6:17-18 the apostle Paul speaks of how to practically touch the nature of the Word: [17] "And take the helmet of salvation, and the sword of the Spirit, which is the word of God: [18] with all prayer and supplication praying at all times in spirit…" (ASV/literal). The word "with" at the beginning of verse 18 is the Greek preposition *dia* (διά). Here it is used with the genitive case and means *through* or *by means of.* In other words, Paul is revealing how to take the word of God — *by means of* or *through* prayer. It is by means of prayer that we touch the true nature of the Word.

The blending of various ways to contact the Lord

When we spend time with the Lord, often a number of things transpire. To begin with, we may feel burdened to put ourselves aside, with all our preoccupations and anxieties. Then we may be touched to spend some time just feeding upon the Word by actually praying over a verse or even just a phrase from a verse. Following this we may sense the need to wait upon the Lord quietly, allowing the love-life of the Triune God to be cultivated within our hearts (Gal. 4:6; Rom. 5:5). Thus, spending time with the Lord may include a blend of several different ways we contact the Lord. The main point during this time is that nothing would become a mere routine or ritual. Whatever we may practice while spending time with the Lord, the purpose is to bring us into God Himself, to have direct contact with Him in our spirit (John 4:24). It is this contact that nourishes us, supplies us, and transforms us.

6

Spending Time with the Lord Early in the Morning

"It is a good thing to let prayer be the first business in the morning and the last in the evening. Guard yourself against such false and deceitful thoughts that keep whispering: Wait a while. In an hour or so I will pray. I must first finish this or that. Thinking such thoughts we get away from prayer into other things that will hold us and involve us till the prayer of the day comes to naught."

– Martin Luther

Rising up early in the morning

In spending time with the Lord another important area to observe is how the Lord practiced rising up early in the morning to be alone with the Father. In considering this we must read Mark 1:35, "And in the early morning, while it was still dark, He arose and went out and departed to a lonely place, and was praying there." The context of this verse indicates that at this particular time the Lord's responsibilities and ministry demands were quite heavy. The night before, He had ministered to virtually the entire city after the sun had gone down (Mark 1:32-34). He was under the pressure of caring for others' needs and sicknesses. There was also the presence of demonic activity in the ones coming to Him. Even His living situation was somewhat inconvenient. He was not in His own home where He could have more easily found a private place to pray. Yet despite His environment and unsettled circumstances, He rose up very early to spend time with the Father in prayer.

The Lord's earthly example of rising early to make time to be with the Father despite His full schedule should help us discern the still small voice in our spirit. That voice, morning by morning, calls us to rise up and spend time with the Lord (Isa. 50:4). That voice is the same life that in the Gospels practiced early rising to fellowship with the Father. Now that life is in our spirit — still needing to spend time with the Father. The Lord was very definite concerning His time with the Father early in the morning. We also need to be definite in this matter if we want to be persons who satisfy the inner requirement of the Lord's life in us.

It is so encouraging to realize that the early-rising life has been received by us *with much grace* (1 Cor. 15:10). This means that spending time with the Lord by rising early is a matter of depending upon the energizing work of the resurrected Christ within us. We cooperate with that grace by choosing morning by morning to rise up early to spend time with Him.

Watchman Nee's testimony, in his book *A Living Sacrifice,* is very helpful concerning this matter of early rising:

> Let me quote the words of Miss Groves, a coworker of Miss M. E. Barber, who has helped us

> greatly. She stated that the first choice giving evidence of one's love towards the Lord is the choice between one's bed and the Lord. If one chooses to love his bed more, he sleeps longer; but if he chooses to love his Lord more, he will rise up a little earlier. She spoke these words to me in 1921, but I still sense the freshness of them today. Yes, a man has to choose between the bed and the Lord. If you love your bed more, sleep on longer; but if you love the Lord more, you must rise up earlier.

We must accept the fact that the Lord's life within us is "our life" according to Colossians 3:4. Regardless of how we feel, when we received Christ we received an early-rising life (Mark 1:35), a prayer life (Heb. 7:16, 25), a love-life (Gal. 4:6), a fellowshipping life (1 John 1:3), and a feasting-upon-the-Word life (1 Pet. 2:2-3). These are the main features of this life that has now become "our life." If we follow this life every morning by rising a little earlier, we will discover that early in the morning there is a special capacity to enjoy the Lord.

The children of Israel experienced a special capacity to collect and enjoy manna early in the morning before the sun became hot (Exo. 16:12, 21). So also in our experience of the Lord's life, there is a special capacity early in the morning to experience and know the Lord, who is the true manna (John 6:32-35). I cannot fully explain or tell you why, but according to my experience there is a greater capacity to hear His voice and receive His impressions early in the morning. I have found that there is a special portion of the enjoyment of the

Lord in the early morning that is different from any other time.

Practicing withdrawing

Another marked feature of how the Lord spent time with the Father was that He practiced withdrawing into the wilderness to pray. The Lord not only rose up early in the morning to be with the Father, but also on many occasions during the day and night He withdrew from the crowds privately to pray. Luke 5:15-17 says, [15] "Then the report went around concerning Him all the more; and great multitudes came together to hear, and to be healed by Him of their infirmities. [16] But He Himself *was* withdrawing in the wilderness and *was* praying.... [17] And the power of the Lord *was* present to heal them." The repetition of the Greek imperfect tense (a tense that shows continuous action in the past), translated as "was" in verses 16 and 17, clearly shows that the Lord's power to heal was in direct proportion to the time He was spending withdrawing to pray. A paraphrase of this portion might help to grasp the sense of the passage: "He Himself was continuously withdrawing in the wilderness and was continuously praying . . . and as a result, the power of the Lord was continuously with Him to heal."

The Lord's practice of withdrawing reveals how much He was actually dependent upon continuous supply to meet His present needs. Even the Lord Jesus Himself needed fresh supply, fresh infusion, and fresh energy imparted into His humanity in order to live a life expressing God. The way He received these fresh supplies was by His practice of withdrawing to spend time with the Father in prayer. By this we can see that the Lord did not live trusting in His divinity to carry Him through His human existence. In His humanity, He needed to withdraw to spend time with the Father for His daily life. If He as the very Son of God depended upon this time, how much more do we need to practice withdrawing in order to be continuously supplied by the divine life.

We must realize that all the pressures we face in our environments are continuous calls to us to spend more time with the Lord. Even our fleshly disposition with its negative reactions, lusts, and moods is a call and a sign that we need to withdraw and pray.

The apostle Paul also faced many difficult situations, such as the one described in 2 Corinthians 1:8: "For we do not want you to be ignorant, brethren, of our trouble which came to us in Asia: that we were burdened beyond measure, above strength, so that we despaired even of life." Here Paul not only had to face a desperate environment, but he also had to handle his reactions of despair to the environment. Yet in the following verses he could testify that God would deliver him by means of prayer and petition (2 Cor. 1:9-11). Brothers and sisters, we must see that the practice of withdrawing to pray and spend time with the Lord should increasingly become a normal part of our Christian life.

The Greek word for withdraw, *hupochoreo* (ὑποχωρέω), in Luke 5:16 is a compound word made up of one preposition meaning *under* and another preposition meaning *apart*. The combination of these two words indicates that the Lord withdrew into privacy. He separated Himself "apart" in privacy to be with the Father. If we desire to cultivate our love-life with the Lord, we will surely discover the Lord Himself moving in us, prodding us to withdraw from all the empty talk and looseness in our living in order to spend more time with Him.

To practice withdrawing we need a vision before us — a vision of the kind of life the Lord Jesus lived on this earth spending time with the Father. He was continuously withdrawing to cultivate and nourish His life with the Father. This is how He expressed God. And this is the life that is now within us. It is a life of withdrawing. This life is a life of feeding upon the Word. This life is a life that gets up early to be with the Father. It is a life that practices withdrawing. This is the life that dwells within us.

So we need to pay attention to the Lord's speaking to us about our schedules, our daily living, and our priorities. We will never be a satisfied person unless we satisfy the inner demand of Christ, who is "our life," to spend time enjoying God. We need to spend time for this love-life and relationship between the Father and the Son to be cultivated within our hearts until we are a reproduction of Christ. The Spirit of His Son is in our hearts crying, "Abba, Father," loving the Father. It is in this triune flow of love that we spend time with Him and enjoy Him.

Do not mourn over yourself. Do not waste time taking condemnation and looking at your condition. Enjoy the Person in whom the Father delights. Just say, "O Father, You delight in Your Son! Look at His blood! Look at His righteousness! Look at His worthiness! Look at what He has attained and accomplished! Father, You cannot turn away the presence of Your Son. Nothing can separate me from Your love which is in Christ Jesus my Lord" (Rom. 8:38-39). In this way we leave our preoccupation with ourself and enjoy this Person. Praise the Lord!

7

Spending Time with the Lord in Prayer

"Prayer is a great mystery. For here we see a principle of God's working, which is, that God's people must pray before God Himself will rise up and work: His will is only to be realized through the prayers of those who belong to Him: the prayers of the believers are to accomplish His will: God will not fulfill His will alone: He will perform only after His people show their sympathy in prayers.

Such being the case, it can therefore be said that prayer is none other than an act of the believer working together with God. Prayer is the union of the believer's thought with the will of God. The prayer which a believer utters on earth is but the voicing of the Lord's will in heaven. Prayer is not the expressing of our wish for God to yield to our petition and fill up our selfish desire. It is not a forcing of the Lord to change His will and perform what He is unwilling to do. No, prayer is simply speaking out the will of God through the mouth of the believer. Before God, the believer asks in prayer for the Lord's will to be done."

– Watchman Nee

One of the most striking examples in the Gospels showing *how* the Lord Jesus spent time with the Father is the record of His spending a whole night in prayer. In Luke 6:12 we read, "Now it came to pass in those days that He went out to the mountain to pray, and continued all night in prayer to God." The last phrase, "in prayer to God," may be translated more literally "in the prayer *of* God." Although most versions of the Bible translate the phrase as an objective genitive — "in prayer *to* God," it is equally proper to translate it as a subjective genitive — "in the prayer *of* God." This simply means that in the prayer, God is not only the object to pray to (*to* God) but He is also the source of the prayer itself (*of* God).

In his *Commentary on the Gospel of Luke*, Frederick L. Godet brings out the more literal translation of Luke 6:12: "The term προσευχὴ τοῦ θεοῦ, literally, *prayer of God*, is also a unique expression in the New Testament. It does not denote any special request, but a state of wrapt contemplation of God's presence, a prayer arising out of the most profound communion with Him." Such a unique description of the Lord's all-night vigil in prayer discloses something of what took place during His prolonged and concentrated time with the Father. "The prayer of God" indicates that in and as a result of His "profound communion" with the Father, the Lord merged with the burden and prayer of God. He so allowed the Father to pass through Him during His communion and fellowship with Him that He became perfectly one with God. He merged with God. This meant God could pass through Him unhindered. He was emptied of self and completely open to the flow of prayer coming directly from God.

Allow God Himself to pass through us

Such a time with the Father, of spending "the whole night in the prayer of God," reveals several crucial points concerning how to spend time with the Lord. First, it reveals that in spending time with the Lord, in order to merge with "the prayer of God," we need to learn to allow God Himself to pass through us. This is fundamental in our fellowship with the Lord. It implies an opening of our entire being to God for Him to flow and pass through us. In the Bible, God is described as a flow; so the nature of our fellowship with Him must be like a flow of "living water" (John 4:10). In Revelation 22:1 the Triune God is described as a flow: "And he showed me a pure river of water of life [the Holy Spirit], clear as crystal, proceeding from the throne of God and of the Lamb..." Jesus declared in John 7:38-39, [38] "He who believes in Me, as the Scripture said, out of his innermost being shall flow rivers of living water. [39] But this He spoke concerning the Spirit, whom those believing in Him would receive." These verses make it clear that to know God is to know Him as a flow.

When we spend time with the Lord, our one need is simply to allow ourselves to be a channel for the Triune God to pass through us. Hallelujah! What a vision of prayer! Spending time with the Lord is a release of our spirit by which we consciously merge with God and allow Him to pass through us. God is a flow! He wants to flow Himself out into our hearts. It is this flow that the apostle Paul describes in Galatians 4:6: "And because you are sons, God has sent forth the Spirit of His

Son into your hearts, crying out, Abba, Father!" Experiencing the reality of this flow is directly related to our merging with it by the active exercise of *our spirit.* The sister-verse to Galatians 4:6 is Romans 8:15, which shows us the need to cooperate with this flow by opening our mouth to contact God: "For you have not received a spirit of slavery leading to fear again, but you have received a spirit of sonship in which we cry out, Abba! Father!" It is in this cry that God witnesses and flows in us. "The Spirit Himself bears witness with our *crying* spirit" (Rom. 8:16).

When we merge with God in this way and allow Him to flow and pass through us, the first benefit we receive is that He imparts His life into our being. Romans 8:11 says, "But if the Spirit of Him who raised Jesus from the dead dwells in you, He who raised Christ from the dead will also give life to your mortal bodies through His Spirit who dwells in you." This indwelling implies an intensive saturation of the Spirit throughout our being, which results in life being imparted into us. Although prayer has its answer, even if there was no answer, by our allowing the Triune God to pass through us we obtain the greatest benefit — the divine life is imparted into us. Thus, when we exercise *our spirit* to cry "Abba, Father" (Rom. 8:15), two things take place in us — the Triune God passes through us, and while passing through He imparts life into our being.

The second benefit of allowing the Triune God to pass through us is that we get cleansed and purified. James 4:8 says, "Draw near to God and He will draw near to you. Cleanse your hands, you sinners; and purify your hearts, you double-minded." This means that in our drawing near, God Himself draws near to us and begins to pass through us. His passing through us has the effect of cleansing and purifying our being. We should not think, however, that such an effect is merely an automatic thing that happens without our cooperation. *Cleanse* and *purify* are both in the imperative mood, indicating our responsibility to confess and deal with the Lord as He passes through us in an inward way. As we merge with God flowing in us, our sins are exposed and cleansed, and our double heart is exposed and purified. If you want to get into the Lord's light, just spend time with the Lord and draw near to Him. Your hands will be cleansed and your heart will be purified. This is the effect of allowing the passing-through of the Triune God.

The third benefit of allowing the Triune God to pass through us is that He sanctifies us; that is, He sets us apart and saturates us with the element of God. We see this in 1 Thessalonians 5:16-19. These verses reveal how the Triune God is interwoven with the various ways we contact the Lord: [16] "Rejoice always, [17] pray without ceasing, [18] in everything give thanks; for this is the will of God in Christ Jesus for you. [19] Do not quench the Spirit." Here we see the Trinity — the Father, the Son, and the Spirit. All Three are related to unceasing prayer, rejoicing, and giving thanks. This shows us that whenever we exercise ourselves in these various ways, we open the way for the Triune God to pass through us. It is by this passing-through of the Triune God that He sanctifies us. The apostle Paul declares in 1 Thessalonians 5:23, "Now may the God of peace Himself *sanctify* you wholly, and may your spirit and soul and body be preserved complete, without blame, at the coming of our Lord Jesus Christ."

Praise the Lord! We receive life, we are cleansed, we are purified, and we are sanctified by allowing the Triune God to pass through us! Just let Him pass through. This is the benefit of praying and of spending time with the Lord—we are joined to the flow of the Triune God. When we pray we allow the Triune God to pass through us, to take care of every one of our needs — to impart life, to cleanse us, to purify us, and to sanctify us. This is the vision we need when we spend time with the Lord. Allow God Himself to pass through you. Just say, "Lord, I want You to pass through me now. I open myself to You from the depths of my being that You may flow in me." Stir up your spirit in this way, and the living water will flow (2 Tim. 1:6-7).

Allow God's intentions to pass through us

Another aspect of merging with the prayer of God is to allow God's intentions to pass through us. Not only God Himself, but God's intentions, must pass through us. In Luke 11:2 when the Lord responded to the disciples concerning prayer, He began by saying, "When you pray, say, Our Father..." Now, we know from other passages of Scripture that no one says "Father" apart from the Son and apart from the Spirit. For example, in John 14:6 the Lord declares, "No one comes to the Father except through Me." And in Ephesians 2:18 Paul says, "For through Him we both have access in one Spirit unto the Father." Just this much in itself stops us, making us realize that the first aspect of prayer is that it is an activity in the Triune God. Thus, when the Lord instructed the disciples to say "Father," He was revealing that prayer is a matter of the Trinity and of our merging with the prayer life of the Trinity.

When the Lord talked about prayer in Luke 11:2, He said, "When you pray, say: Our Father in heaven, hallowed be Your name. Your kingdom come." This means that to pray is to allow God's intentions — "Your name be sanctified; Your kingdom come" — to pass through us. We must see that this is a crucial aspect concerning the prayer of God. When we pray, He passes through us doing all His work. But His intentions must also pass through us. This means we must be persons who pour God's intentions into our being and are purified from other intentions, motives, and goals. Then we are persons who are filled with the intentions of the Triune God. This is the proper understanding of the prayer of God. It is simply God Himself and His intentions passing through us.

How much have God's intentions passed through us? Do we know what it means to pray, "Lord, Your name be sanctified. Lord, Your kingdom come"? For this kind of prayer we need light and revelation. So we should pray, "Lord, fill me with Your intentions." This is how Paul prayed for the believers in Ephesians 3:9-11. In his prayer he opened up the vision of God's intention: [9] "And to bring to light what is the administration of the mystery which for ages has been hidden in God, who created all things; [10] in order that the manifold wisdom of God might now be made known through the church to the rulers and the authorities in the heavenly places. [11] This was in accordance with the eternal purpose which He carried out in Christ Jesus our Lord."

In these verses Paul brings to light God's intention in the universe — that which had its beginning in eternity past and will be consummated in eternity future, and which is now being made known to the rulers and the authorities in the heavenlies. And what is God's intention? God's eternal purpose and intention is that His manifold wisdom would be made known through the church.

Immediately following the declaration that God's intention was carried out in Christ Jesus our Lord, Paul says in verse 12, "In whom . . ." Paul knew exactly where he was. He was in the Second in the Godhead. In whom? Christ Jesus our Lord. He merged with the prayer life of the Triune God. And in this One, Christ Jesus our Lord, "we have boldness and access in confidence through the faith of Him." This means that Paul's boldness and confidence and access to pray issued from God's intentions pulsating in his being!

When Paul spoke in this way—"boldness and access in confidence through the faith of Him"—he was building one word upon another. It was as though he had mounted up to the heavens to command the whole universe to come under God's administration. Here Paul was not engaged in prayer to fulfill his own needs and desires. Although God does answer our personal requests, we need a higher vision so that we can pray with God's needs and intentions in our being. This is the way Paul prayed. He fully merged in his prayer with the eternal intentions of the Triune God.

Then in Ephesians 3:13 Paul told the believers not to be anxious about him and the trials he was passing through. He referred to what he was experiencing as "my tribulations for you, which is your glory." Then in verse 14 he continued, "For this reason I bow my knees to the Father." And in verse 16 he proceeded right to the heart of the matter, praying that the saints would have the kind of experience that would make them the ones fulfilling God's intention. He prayed that they would be strengthened into the inner man in order that Christ could spread out and make His home in their hearts. From such a spreading of Christ within them, they would be "rooted and grounded in love," and would have the ability to "apprehend with all the saints what is the breadth and length and height and depth, and to know the knowledge-surpassing love of Christ," that they could be "filled with all the fullness of God" (vv. 17-19).

In verse 20 Paul continued to ascend even higher, declaring, "But to Him who is able to do superabundantly above all that we ask or think, according to the power which operates in us." And in verse 21 he reached the peak: "To Him be the glory in the church and in Christ Jesus unto all the generations of the age of the ages. Amen." God's intentions just passed through that brother! Oh, that the saints could experience such a dispensing of the Trinity — the Father, the Son, and the Spirit — into and through their being. Paul uses all Three interchangeably here: that you may be strengthened into the inner man through His *Spirit,* that *Christ* may make His home, that *God* would be all in all.

So we can see that Paul was a brother under the light and revelation of God's intentions. As believers we need the same vision of prayer in order that God, with His intentions, may pass through us. This is the vision we need in spending time with the Lord in order that we could more adequately merge with "the prayer of God."

Allowing God's desires to pass through us

When we pray, not only God's intentions but also His desires must pass through us. This point is revealed in 1 Timothy 2:1, where Paul says, "Therefore, I exhort first of all that supplications, prayers, intercessions, and giving of thanks be made for all men." Then verse 4 speaks of our Savior God, "who desires all men to be saved and to come to the full knowledge of the truth." This means that God's express desire is for all men to be saved. So when we pray, we not only touch the larger scale of God's intentions for the church and the kingdom, but we also allow God's desires for all men to pass through us. This includes God's desires for everyone in *your* life: co-workers, neighbors, classmates, the mailman, the checker at the grocery store, the person you met at the bus stop, as well as your family members and relatives. Paul says that first of all there must be supplications and prayers, intercessions, and thanksgivings made for all men. Thus, in spending time with the Lord we can allow God's desires for others to pass through us.

Effectual prayer is made up of desire. For example, we may

want to see someone saved. Yet if in our prayer our own heart is not deeply moved for that one, such a prayer will never move the heart of God. If we ourselves do not possess the desire to see someone saved, how could God's desire ever be released in our prayer? Paul illustrated this principle when he said, "Therefore, *we* are ambassadors for Christ, as though God were pleading *through us: we* implore on Christ's behalf, Be reconciled to God" (2 Cor. 5:20). This indicates that God's desires are not merely kept within Himself. They need a human channel to pass through. God's desire to see the lost saved must be located within our very being. God's desire must become *our* desire, culminating in our persevering in prayer for them.

First Timothy 2:4 also shows us that God desires not only that all men be saved, but also that all would "come to the full knowledge of the truth." This desire is related to all believers. It is God's express desire that all His children come to the full knowledge of the truth. The full knowledge of the truth is found in Paul's prayer in Ephesians 1:17, in which he requests that believers may be given "a spirit of wisdom and revelation in the full knowledge of Him." It is also found in Paul's prayer in Colossians 1:9, in which he asks that believers "may be filled with the full knowledge of His will in all spiritual wisdom and understanding." The "full knowledge" in both prayers is related to God's eternal thought and purpose of obtaining a glorious church that fully expresses Him. This means that when we pray for believers, we need to allow God's desire that they come to the full knowledge of the truth to pass through us. Spending adequate time with the Lord makes it possible for us to merge with this kind of burden for all God's children.

Allowing God's sovereign designs to pass through us

Another result of spending time with the Lord is allowing God's sovereign designs for believers to pass through us. This is a definite aspect of the prayer of God. God has unique designs with every one of us — to so arrange our environment and circumstances that we would be brought on to conformity to the image of His Son (Rom. 8:29). Yet due to our weakness, we do not know how to pray as we ought. Thus, in Romans 8:26-27 there is the intercession of the Spirit with groanings which cannot be uttered. Verse 26 says, "And in like manner the Spirit also joins in to help us in our weakness; for we do not know for *what* we should pray as is fitting..." In the original Greek, the definite article "the" is before the word "what," meaning literally that "we do not know *the what* we should pray as is fitting."

Now, what is *the what*? According to the context of this passage, *the what* refers to the specific things that are divinely arranged to take place in our environment. Whatever these things turn out to be, they are working together for good — to cause us to be more conformed to the image of God's Son. They may include what we would consider negative things. They may be specific situations that are contrary to what we would choose or prefer. Hebrews 12 tells us that these environmental things are the Lord's discipline in our lives. The discipline may come in the form of a physical problem. It may be a family problem. It may be a job problem. It may be some pressure in your marriage relationship. It may be pressure in other relationships. The Lord knows exactly what every one of us needs.

We each need a certain kind of environment, a certain kind of situation, that will affect us a certain way in order to press us to the Spirit and cause us to wash our hands from our sins, our flesh, our inertia. But we do not know how to pray like this. You do not know how to pray for me, and I do not know how to pray for you. We do not pray, "Lord, grant some negative things to happen to this brother in his home this week. Lord, grant the loss of a job to this sister. Lord, cause this school to turn down this person's application." We do not pray this way. As we are praying, what we find in our hearts is, "Lord, take us all on with You!" Yet within this prayer there is an unutterable groan. It is the burden and the groaning of the Spirit searching our divided and distracted hearts, searching out where we are as Romans 8:26-27 says, [26] "The Spirit Himself makes intercession for us with groanings which cannot be uttered. [27] Now He who searches the hearts knows what the mind of the Spirit is, because He makes intercession for the saints according to the will of God."

Although we do not know precisely how to pray, the Lord knows how to read the groans of the Spirit passing through His saints. We may only be able to pray, "O God." But the Lord reads the unutterable groan in that prayer. Then Romans 8:28 says, "And we know that God causes all things to work together for good." The "all things" in this verse turn out to be the answer to "the what" prayers in Romans 8:26-27. This means that none of the things in our environment are accidents. Everything has happened due to the prayers of the Spirit with His unutterable groans. He is accurately praying in us for all the believers "according to God," not according to our idea of a good life, nor according to what we think we need.

So whatever has been apportioned to us in our environment is not accidental. Yet if we lack this kind of understanding, we may blame the things happening to us or blame others and unwittingly be in rebellion to God. If we find ourselves full of complaining and blaming, we should do one thing — draw a circle around ourselves and deal directly with God. We dare not put the blame on anything — the past, any person, or whatever. Then we will get the most out of our environment and be conformed to the image of God's Son.

Our environment is under the sovereign hand of God. But even more, it is a direct answer to prayer, because some are allowing the unutterable groans of the Spirit to pass through them, releasing the designs of God for all His saints. This is the vision we need in order to enrich the time we spend with the Lord in "the prayer of God." It is an awesome thought that God uses us as channels and allows His intentions, desires, and designs to pass through us. The more time we spend with the Lord, the more opportunity we give God to have a way on this earth through us to accomplish His purpose.

8

Learning the Nature of the Lord's Voice

"Learn ever to read the book of the new covenant in the new covenant Spirit. . . . When God says, I will put My law in their inward parts, and write it in their hearts, He engages that the words of His Holy Book shall no longer be mere outward teaching, but that what they command shall be our very disposition and delight, wrought in us as a birth and a life by the Holy Spirit. Every word of the new covenant then becomes a divine assurance of what may be obtained by the Holy Spirit's working. . . . It then is a word that works effectually in them that believe, giving within the heart the actual possession of the very grace of which the Word has spoken."

– Andrew Murray

Introduction

According to the Lord's own words in John 10:27, His sheep hear His voice and they follow Him. Thus, as believers, we need to understand what it means to follow our Shepherd by hearing His voice and inner speaking. His voice in us is a present reality and touches the details of our daily life. As we hear His voice and go along with it, we become partakers of the Lord, and God's purpose of transforming us into the image of His Son progresses in us.

In spending time with the Lord, we discover that our God is a living, talking, and speaking God. He even identifies Himself as the Word. Concerning the Lord Jesus, John 1:1 says, "In the beginning was the Word, and the Word was with God, and the Word was God." He is the *logos*, or Word. That means Christ as the Word is God's speech and utterance. Now this One as the *logos* has entered into our being. He comes into us as the Word, with His voice and speaking. Therefore, we need to understand the nature of His voice.

The Nature of the Lord's Voice under the Old Covenant

The ten words written on tablets of stone

To fully appreciate the nature of the Lord's voice under the new covenant, we need to see the nature of His voice under the old covenant. In Old Testament times under the old covenant, God did speak. His voice was there. One of the ways God spoke was in the ten words written on the tablets of stone, that is, in the ten commandments. In Deuteronomy 10:4, most of the Bible translations (at least in the margin) do not say "ten commandments" but "ten words." God spoke ten words that revealed His nature and the kind of God He is.

The kind of commands we give reveals the kind of persons we are. For example, if I am a loose person, my commands will be loose. If I am a strict person, my commands will be strict. The kind of person I am will be expressed in the kind of commandments I give. Thus, the kind of God we have is revealed in His commandments. That God would command, "You shall have no other gods before Me," indicates that He wants our affection exclusively. God wants our heart. Similarly, the fact that He would command, "You shall not kill," reveals that our God is a God of life and love. He gives His commandments to reveal something of what kind of God He is and what kind of nature He has. The ten commandments also reveal how much we fall short of what God is. They reveal to us that we are sinners and that we need Christ. Accordingly, they lead us to Christ.

The main point under the old covenant was that when God spoke, His voice was written in the tablets of stone. Though under the old covenant His voice was true and revealed His holy and loving nature, it could not supply the life that His voice can now supply under the new covenant (cf. Gal. 3:21; John 5:24-25).

In the holy of holies

Exodus 25 gives us another picture of how God spoke under the old covenant. This chapter records that He spoke in the holy of holies, where He met with man from above the blood-sprinkled mercy seat and between the two cherubim. There, He came to meet with the children of Israel. God said to Moses, "There I will meet with you, and I will speak with you" (Exo. 25:22). Thus, the words of God were coming forth in the holy of holies. This place of God's speaking was known in the Old Testament as the oracle of God (1 Kings 8:6, ASV).

Under the old covenant, God's speaking was there in the ten words on the tablets of stone, and His speaking was there in the holy of holies. Both these instances of God's speaking revealed His holiness and glory. Nevertheless, the Lord's voice under the old covenant was not yet of the nature of an *inward* communication of Himself. Rather, God's speaking during the Old Testament period was of the nature of an *outward* communication of His desires and will.

In many portions and ways through the prophets

Hebrews 1:1 also gives a good summary of the nature of God's speaking under the old covenant: "God, who at various times and in different ways spoke in time past to the fathers by the prophets . . ." God spoke in many different ways in the Old Testament. For example, sometimes He spoke in a vision, sometimes in a dream. God spoke to Daniel and to King Nebuchadnezzar in these ways.

We see then that under the old covenant God was speaking in many different ways: through the law in the tablets of stone, in the speaking-place from above the mercy seat, through visions, through dreams, through prophets receiving a word from the Lord and speaking it to the people. In all these ways, the people had to depend primarily upon another person, such as a prophet, to hear God's direct speaking. Thus, the kind of speaking under the old covenant, although true and proper, was still outward in nature.

THE NATURE OF THE LORD'S VOICE UNDER THE NEW COVENANT

In His Son

Under the new covenant the speaking of the Lord, or the voice of the Lord, is of a different nature. Hebrews 1:1-2 says, [1] "God, who at various times and in different ways spoke in time past to the fathers by the prophets, [2] has in these last days spoken to us *in the Son,* whom He has appointed heir of all things, through whom also He made the universe." *The New Translation* by J. N. Darby omits the definite article "the" in the phrase "in the Son." This omission is in keeping with the structure of the literal Greek text. Thus, it reads "in Son." This same grammatical construction is found in John 4:24 with the words "God is Spirit." The definite article is absent in both cases. In Hebrews 1:1, the phrase "the prophets" has the definite article. Thus, in verse 2 you would expect to read, "has at the last of these days spoken to us in *the Son.*" But it does not say *the Son;* it says "in Son" or "in a Son." This is because in the Greek language when the nature of something is being emphasized, the definite article is usually omitted. Here the emphasis is on the nature of Christ as a Son. God's speaking now, under the new covenant, is of the nature of a son's relationship with a father.

The description of Christ as "a Son" implies a relationship of life and love. First, a son is one who has the life of his father. For example, I have two sons. They have my life. I begat them. Thus, being a son has to do with a life-relationship. When the writer of Hebrews says that God has spoken to us in a Son, this means that God's speaking to us is bound up in our life-relationship and fellowship with the Son. It reveals that the nature of God's voice in us is related to our participation in and enjoyment of the life of the Son. In other words, the more we learn how to enjoy and partake of Christ Himself as life, the more we will hear the Lord's voice. It may even be said that the Lord's voice in us is a life-voice, as John 5:25-26 reveals: [25] "Most assuredly, I say to you, the hour is coming, and now is, when the dead will hear the voice of the Son of God; and those who hear will live. [26] For as the Father has life in Himself, so He has granted the Son to have life in Himself."

Second, a son not only has a life-relationship, but also a love-relationship. Love is the realm in which the Son of God lives and exists. The Father loves the Son, and the Son loves the Father. To say that God has spoken to us "in a Son" definitely implies that God's speaking in us is related to our love-relationship with the Lord. As we enjoy the fellowship of life, and as we cultivate a love-relationship with Him in our heart, we will spontaneously become acquainted with His voice in us (cf. 1 John 5:2-4). Out of the flow of life and love comes much inner speaking. To know the Lord as life and love is to know His voice in us. This is the nature of the Lord's voice under the new covenant.

Upon the tablets of the heart

Christ as the *Word / logos* (John 1:1) dwelling within us speaks in the form of spiritual writing upon our hearts. Indeed, this is one of the main distinguishing marks of the new covenant in contrast with the old covenant. God's law is no longer being written on tablets of stone but on the fleshly tablets of our hearts. In 2 Corinthians 3:3 Paul says, "You are manifestly an epistle of Christ, ministered by us, written not with ink but by the Spirit of the living God, not on tablets of stone but on tablets of flesh, that is, of the heart." Thus, to know the Lord's voice within us is to understand the way His voice manifests itself — by the Spirit's writing upon our hearts.

The subject of the Spirit's writing is *the law of God* as it is described by the Lord Himself in Matthew 5—7. Paul describes this same subject in Romans 8:4-5: [4] "That *the righteous requirement of the law* might be fulfilled *in us* who do not walk according to the flesh but according to the spirit. [5] For those who live according to the flesh set their minds on the things of the flesh, but those who live according to the spirit, the things of the spirit." The righteous requirement of the law is what the Lord taught in Matthew 5—7 in what is commonly called the Sermon on the Mount. Now this uplifted law is being written upon our hearts by the Spirit. It is this Spirit-writing that constitutes the Lord's voice within us.

The evidence of our hearing the Lord's voice is both the consciousness we have within our hearts as well as the inclination of our hearts. For example, the very consciousness and prompting in us forbidding us to take a certain course of action or hold a certain attitude is His speaking within. The consciousness itself is the Lord's voice. This kind of consciousness may also be understood as a consciousness of life, because the nature of the consciousness is an inner awareness that is being supplied to us by the life of God. If we cooperate with this consciousness, or in other words, if we listen to the Lord's voice within, and by faith obey His forbidding feeling, we will unlock the floodgate of the Spirit of life into our whole being. It is important to know that His voice always comes with the supply of His presence and grace.

The uniqueness of our new covenant relationship with the Lord is this: it is not a matter of our keeping outward commands, but of discovering His voice as an inner consciousness. Thus, it is not being outwardly *told* what to do; it is being *prompted* from within concerning what to do. So expect the Lord's voice to come from within you. And the way you will discover His voice is by His inner operation that manifests itself by inward promptings. What is important then is how we respond to these promptings.

Let me give an illustration. The most basic function of a PC computer is a little blinking "C" at the bottom of the screen known as the "C prompt." Its appearance on the screen tells you that the computer is operating and is prompting you to enter a command. The prompt is the computer's way of speaking to you; it is the computer's voice. Of course, when you respond to the prompt by entering a command, you open up a wealth of information on the screen. An entire computer world is instantly available to you by simply responding to the "prompt."

In the same way, we as believers, indwelt by the life of God, have promptings within us. These promptings are the Lord's way of speaking to us. They *are* the Lord's voice. They are telling us that God is operating in us to open up all the riches of His life to our inward parts. However, to get the benefit of

God's life within we need to respond properly to the prompting. In our daily life, when we say "Amen" to the prompting within and go along with it, we are obeying the voice of the Lord.

This prompting is what Paul refers to in Philippians 2:12-14: [12]"Therefore, my beloved, as you have always obeyed, not as in my presence only, but now much more in my absence, work out your own salvation with fear and trembling; [13]for it is God who operates in you both to will and to do for His good pleasure. [14]Do all things without murmuring and reasoning." In the first part of verse 12, Paul mentions the word *obey*. In Greek this is a compound word formed by the two words "hear" and "under." Thus, to obey means "to be under a hearing." Hearing the Lord's voice is integral to obeying or following Him, even as He indicated in John 10:27: "My sheep *hear* My voice, and I know them, and they follow Me."

To hear the Lord under the new covenant means to recognize promptings within our heart. The prompting is God Himself operating within us. It is this prompting that Paul refers to in Philippians 2:13: "For it is God who operates in you both to will and to do for His good pleasure." When we respond positively to the prompting, we are actually obeying Him. It is at the point of obeying Him that we need to see the difference between Old Testament and New Testament obedience. Old Testament obedience is man responding to the outward law of God without the supply of life that is necessary to carry it out (Gal. 3:21). New Testament obedience is man responding to God from the very responses and promptings inwardly produced by God Himself out of the riches and supply of His grace.

It is by grace that God authors and produces within us the promptings to Himself. Then He supplies grace once again at every point that we obey His voice and respond to His inner promptings. This is what is meant in John 1:16: "And of His fullness we have all received, and grace *for* grace" (or, "grace *in exchange for* grace" — Gk. *anti* / ἀντί). When we obey by saying "Amen" to His speaking, we are not carrying out an act of obedience from our own energy or strength. We are exchanging the grace of His promptings for a fresh supply of grace to work out those promptings in our practical experience. Obedience under the new covenant is a step of faith to open ourselves to the flow of God's grace to once again supply us with Himself. Thus, to hear His voice is not to come under a demand of the law. Rather, it is to hear a call to enjoy a fresh supply of grace.

The Lord's voice is located in the region of our heart. Hebrews 3:7-8 tells us, [7] "Therefore, as the Holy Spirit says: Today, if you will hear His voice, [8] do not harden your hearts as in the rebellion, in the day of trial in the wilderness." The voice of God speaks in our hearts. When the Lord is speaking we can either constrict and harden our heart so that it is not soft and pliable to His voice, or we can hear His voice and soften our heart and go along with that voice. This is the way we interact with the Lord's voice under the new covenant.

Imparted and written upon our inward parts

Further development of the truth concerning the Lord's voice is found in Hebrews 8:10-11: [10] "For this is the covenant that I will make with the house of Israel after those days, says the LORD: I will impart My laws in their mind and write them on their hearts; and I will be their God, and they shall be My people. [11] None of them shall teach his neighbor, and none his brother, saying, 'Know the LORD,' for all shall know Me, from the least of them to the greatest of them." These two verses are a quotation from Jeremiah 31:33-34. Again, the uniqueness of the new covenant is in the imparting of His laws into our mind and the actual inscribing of them on our heart. This shows that the voice of the Lord is in our thoughts and in our heart. His voice is in our desires, in our feelings, in that inner operation of being prompted with an impulse concerning something. His voice is also in the inclination of our will. The Lord's voice under the new covenant is directly present within the heart of every believer. This is the nature of His speaking.

Sometimes the Lord's voice comes in the form of a question, such as, What are you doing here? or, Where are you going? For example, one day the prophet Elijah was sulking because Jezebel was seeking his life (1 Kings 19:2). Yes, Elijah was truly a mighty man of God. He had already caused fire from heaven to come down and consume an offering, thus exposing the falseness of the prophets of Baal and exonerating and vindicating the living God (1 Kings 18:19-39). But when he heard the report that Jezebel wanted to kill him, he ran for his life. Eventually, his flight ended with his hiding in a cave.

In 1 Kings 19:9-13, we read the details of Elijah's encounter with the Lord's voice: [9] "And there he went into a cave, and spent the night in that place; and behold, the word of the LORD came to him, and He said to him, 'What are you doing here,

Elijah?' [10] So he said, 'I have been very zealous for the LORD God of hosts; for the children of Israel have forsaken Your covenant, torn down Your altars, and killed Your prophets with the sword. I alone am left; and they seek to take my life.' [11] Then He said, 'Go out, and stand on the mountain before the LORD.' And behold, the LORD passed by, and a great and strong wind tore into the mountains and broke the rocks in pieces before the LORD, but the LORD was not in the wind; and after the wind an earthquake, but the LORD was not in the earthquake; [12] and after the earthquake a fire, but the LORD was not in the fire; and after the fire a still small voice. [13] So it was, when Elijah heard it, that he wrapped his face in his mantle and went out and stood in the entrance of the cave. And suddenly a voice came to him, and said, 'What are you doing here, Elijah?'" This story illustrates how the Lord is in the still small voice. In the original Hebrew language it means "a delicate whispering voice." The Lord was in that whisper. God's speaking was in that still small voice, and it was in the form of a question, "What are you doing here?"

Maybe you have found yourself in "a cave" at some time. Perhaps you went to the cave of a movie theater, and while you were watching all the defiling things on the screen, there arose a consciousness within you in the form of a question, "What are you doing here?" You can be sure that that was God talking to you. That is the way His voice speaks — right inside of you, within your own consciousness.

In Genesis 3, God approached Adam in the same way. After Adam had hidden himself from the presence of the Lord, God came to him asking the question, "Where are you?" Of course,

God already knew where Adam was, but Adam still had to admit to himself and to God where he was. Sometimes in our lives, when we are living in vanity, when we are in our own little world with our own self-centered goals and aims, there comes a consciousness within us with words that form in our own thoughts saying, "Where am I? What am I doing with my life? Where will my life end up?" It may seem like our own mind talking, but we must realize that God's voice comes to us as He is writing it into our consciousness — into our own thoughts and heart. God is talking to us through our own consciousness. This way of speaking is according to the new covenant. He is not merely talking to us, but He is infusing and supplying into us the very thing He is speaking about.

We probably do not realize how much of the Lord's speaking we, as believers, have in our daily life. For example, you may remember someone during the day. Perhaps as you are washing the dishes, you think about that person. Actually it is the Lord speaking to you, putting that person on your heart so that you would pray for him or give him a phone call. It is in these practical ways that Christ manifests Himself in us as our life.

In his letters to the churches and to individuals, Paul describes his experiences of having the Lord's speaking. In 2 Timothy 1:3-5 he says, [3]"I thank God, whom I serve with a pure conscience, as my forefathers did, as without ceasing I *remember* you in my prayers night and day, [4]greatly desiring to see you, *remembering* your tears, that I may be filled with joy, [5] when I call to *remembrance* the genuine faith that is in you, which dwelt first in your grandmother Lois and your mother Eunice, and I am persuaded is in you also." Paul illustrates in these verses that the Lord's voice speaking to him is in and through his thoughts. It is in the normal avenues and channels of his being. The Lord's speaking to Paul came in the form of his remembrance. The remembrance of Timothy was a call to pray for Timothy. This example out of Paul's life corresponds to God's new covenant way of imparting His laws into our mind and inscribing them upon our heart (Heb. 8:10).

When we understand this new covenant way of God's speaking, we must confess that we all have heard more of His voice in our daily life than we realized. For example, God's speaking has come to us many times in the form of desires within us. We may have a desire to go to a church meeting. That very desire within us is God's speaking in the form of an inclination inscribed on our heart.

Also, the Lord's voice often comes in the way of His bringing something to mind. For example, in Matthew 5:23 the Lord says, "Therefore if you bring your gift to the altar, and there remember that your brother has something against you. . ." In other words, while you are fellowshipping with the Lord, something comes to mind. You remember your brother. When it comes to mind, that is the Lord speaking to you. Thus, we can see how simple and intimate is the Lord's voice *to* us and *in* us under the new covenant. His speaking is imparted into our mind.

Through our environment

Often in our experience the Lord's voice in us encounters

a deaf or indifferent ear. When this occurs, the Lord has a way to turn up the volume of His speaking. According to the Scriptures, His way is to use our environment and circumstances to intensify His inner speaking. This is the spiritual principle of discipline and chastisement in the lives of all God's children (cf. Heb. 12:5-9). The effect that God's discipline has on our ability to hear the Lord's voice is clearly seen in Isaiah 30:20-21: [20]"And though the Lord gives you the bread of adversity and the water of affliction, yet your teachers will not be moved into a corner anymore, but your eyes shall see your teachers. [21] Your ears shall hear a word behind you, saying, 'This is the way, walk in it,' whenever you turn to the right hand or whenever you turn to the left."

When the Lord gives us the bread of *adversity* and the water of *affliction,* He does it to get our attention, that we may hear His voice. Adversity and affliction are described as teachers that are not hidden in a corner anymore. Indeed, our eyes will see our teachers. These teachers are different from brothers and sisters giving us outward instructions. They are like personal tutors that are able to get our attention so that we will listen to the Lord. They are sent by God when all else seems to fail. Under God's sovereignty, the environments of adversity and affliction are used by Him to attain one end — our hearing the Lord's voice.

The effectiveness of environmental discipline in our lives is evidenced by the fact that we eventually do hear a voice behind us saying, "This is the way, walk in it," when we turn to the right or when we turn to the left. This voice keeps us on the straight and narrow way of experiencing Christ. Our tendency is to be side-tracked, turning aside either to the right or to the left. The right and left represent evil, the flesh, the world, or our own independent way (cf. Prov. 4:23-27). If we have learned from our teachers of adversity and affliction, when we are again tempted to turn off the road to the right or left, *we will hear* the Lord speaking through our consciousness, "This is the way (Christ), walk in it (Him)" (cf. Col. 2:6). All of God's discipline in our lives has this one goal — that we would hear the Lord's voice and follow Him.

In the New Testament, Revelation 3:19-20 reveals this same principle of discipline used by God to secure our inner attention to hear His voice. Here the Lord says, [19]"As many as I love, I rebuke and discipline. Therefore be zealous and repent. [20]Behold, I stand at the door and knock. If anyone hears My voice and opens the door, I will come in to him and dine with him, and he with Me." The Lord gives a little rebuking and a little discipline to turn up the volume of His voice. He has already been speaking in us, even standing at the door and knocking; but we have not heard His voice. Now He knocks a little harder through rebuke and discipline. When He says, "If anyone hears My voice," it is as though He is saying, "I spoke to you in a whisper, in a still small voice, but you closed your ears to Me by your reasoning mind. Your own self-centered desires deafened and muffled My voice. But now, through discipline, I have secured My goal in your life. You hear My voice and are opening the door, and I am coming into your heart to set up an inner table where we can feast together — you with Me and I with you."

May the Holy Spirit cause us all to become warm within, so that we all can say, "Lord, thank You that Your voice is so intimate in me all day long." Begin thanking Him for His voice even though you have not obeyed it. Simply say, "Thank You for speaking. Thank You for this consciousness. Thank You, Lord, that You have been speaking in me even though I did not listen." As we begin in this way to enjoy Him and partake of Him, we will find within us godly desires, a Spirit-wrought willingness, and inclinations toward the things of God, which come from God Himself operating in our being. By learning to follow this inner operation, we become, in reality, one of His sheep who hear His voice and follow Him in daily life. This is what it means to experience God's economy, and this is the pathway to God's eternal purpose of conformity to the image of Christ. Amen!

9

Recognizing the Lord's Voice

"God does not cease to speak, but the noise of the world outside us, and the noise of our passions within, prevent our hearing him. We must silence every creature, including self, that we may perceive the ineffable voice of the Bridegroom in the deep stillness of the soul. We must lend an attentive ear, for His voice is soft and still, and is heard only by those who hear nothing else."

– François Fénelon

Hearing and understanding the Lord's voice is a vital and integral part of our daily Christian life. We are actually participating in Christ's own experience described in Isaiah 50:4-5: [4] "The Lord GOD has given Me the tongue of the learned, that I should know how to speak a word in season to him who is weary. *He awakens Me morning by morning, He awakens My ear to hear as the learned.* [5] *The Lord GOD has opened My ear; and I was not rebellious, nor did I turn away.*" The Lord Himself needed to have His ear awakened morning by morning in order to live an obedient life in His humanity. The Lord lives His life in us today in the same way that He lived His life on the earth. Indeed, His human life is being reproduced in us by the Spirit. Thus, we should become more familiar with this aspect of His life so that we can hear and understand His voice in us.

The Lord's voice is like an inner drawing

The Lord's voice in us is described in John's Gospel as an inner drawing. In John 6:37 the Lord says, "All that the Father gives Me will come to Me, and the one who comes to Me I will by no means cast out." And again in verses 44-45 He says, [44] "No one can come to Me unless the Father who sent Me *draws him;* and I will raise him up at the last day. [45] It is written in the prophets, 'And they shall all be taught by God.' Therefore *everyone who has heard* and learned from the Father comes to Me." Thus, to hear God and be taught by God is, in essence, to experience an inward drawing toward the Lord Jesus. That is, this inward speaking is experienced as an attraction toward Christ. This inner drawing indicates His direct speaking to us.

Although I did not realize it at the time, I experienced this inward speaking when I first came to the Lord. After hearing the gospel for the first time, there was a constant inner drawing in me toward Christ. This drawing expressed itself in my curiosity toward the Bible and church history. It also expressed itself through my interest in the girl that later became my wife. She spoke to me about the Lord in a way I had never heard before. The Lord was drawing me to Himself, and this drawing *was* His speaking to me.

The Greek word for draw is *helkuõ* (ἑλκύω) and may be properly understood as a gentle inner persuasion. It is something in you that attracts and persuades you toward the Lord and the things of the Lord. It is the same kind of experience spoken of in Jeremiah 31:3: "The LORD has appeared of old to me, saying: 'Yes, I have loved you with an everlasting love; therefore with lovingkindness I have *drawn* you.' " So the manner of the Lord's speaking is that gentle persuasion of love that draws our hearts to Him.

The speaking of the Lord under the new covenant is an inward drawing resulting from a divine operation in our being. The drawing *is* His speaking. Even though we are sometimes indifferent to that inner drawing, it is still there in us. We can run away from it or we can nurture it. Whatever measure of drawing to the Lord we may have, it is deserving of our thanksgiving. We should say, "Thank You, Lord, for the desire that I find in myself for You." Even a little bit of desire in us for the Lord should be considered His speaking.

His speaking manifests itself by an inward drawing. In other words, He does not normally speak with audible words, telling us what to do or not to do. Rather, He actually imparts into us the very substance and reality of His speaking. For example, if He is speaking to us about "willingness" in an area of our lives, He will incline and draw our hearts in that area. Philippians 2:12-13 makes this clear: [12] "Therefore, my beloved, as you have always obeyed, not as in my presence only, but now much more in my absence, work out your own salvation with fear and trembling; [13] *for it is God who works in you both to will and to do* for His good pleasure." God Himself operates within to produce the willingness and the working. This illustrates that knowing the Lord's voice is related to recognizing His drawing from within our hearts.

The Old Testament example of the Shulammite maiden's request to her bridegroom expresses the same kind of drawing spoken of in the New Testament. In Song of Songs 1:4 the maiden says, "Draw me; we will run after thee" (ASV). When the Lord draws us, we will run after Him. We can be sure that when we find within us that gentle inner drawing toward the Lord, that itself *is* the Lord's speaking to us. By grace He works within us to impart the very reality of the words He speaks. When He calls us to Himself, He makes us feel an inward drawing toward Him, even as He declares in John 12:32: "And I, if I am lifted up from the earth, *will draw all men to Myself.*"

The Lord's voice is like an inner knowing

From John 10 we observe that the Lord's voice in our experience is like an inner knowing. Verses 4-5 say, [4] "And when he brings out his own sheep, he goes before them; and the sheep follow him, for *they know his voice.* [5] Yet they will by no means follow a stranger, but will flee from him, *for they do not know the voice of strangers.*" Also, in verse 14 the Lord says, "I am the good shepherd; and *I know My sheep, and am known by My own.*" This inner knowing of the Lord's voice is similar to experiencing an inner drawing. We are moved and touched from within. In our experience there is a deep inner consciousness and conviction. This means the Lord's voice is written into our very consciousness.

For example, when we received Christ into us, it was

because we were convinced by this inner knowing that we should receive Him. *Outwardly*, we may have *heard* a preacher sharing the gospel, or we may have *read* a tract explaining to our mind the way of salvation. But *inwardly* we *knew* that receiving Christ was the right thing to do. This inner knowing to follow the Lord as our Shepherd is simply His voice speaking in our consciousness.

Our inner knowing of the Lord's voice has a long history. It goes back to eternity past and stretches forward to eternity future. In John 10:3 the Lord says, "the sheep hear his voice; and he calls his own sheep *by name* and leads them out." We must see that the reason He can call His own sheep by name is because in eternity past we were given by the Father to the Son *by name*. He knows us by name. In fact, we were all personal gifts given by the Father to the Son. In John 10:27-29 the Lord says, [27] "My sheep hear My voice, and *I know them*, and they follow Me. [28] And I give them eternal life, and they shall never perish; neither shall anyone snatch them out of My hand. [29] *My Father, who has given them to Me*, is greater than all; and no one is able to snatch them out of My Father's hand." These verses in John 10, together with Hebrews 13:20-21 that speaks of the Lord being the great Shepherd of the sheep in the blood of an eternal covenant, show us something of the substance of our inner knowing of the Lord. Namely, that our inner knowing of His voice *today,* in this period called "time," is our response to the Father and the Son's *eternal* knowing of us. So we can confidently say that we know Him because He first knew us (cf. Gal. 4:9).

The Son willingly took us by name, and then in the eternal covenant He agreed to shepherd us all the way — out of eternity past, through time with all the problems of sin, the flesh, the world, and the devil, and into eternity future. Overcoming all obstacles, He will bring us through, fully conformed to His image.

Furthermore, this inner knowing is a reality to us as Romans 8:16 says, "The Spirit Himself bears witness with our spirit that we are children of God." The Spirit witnessing with our spirit is an inner knowing and consciousness. This is His way of speaking to us in the most intimate and personal manner. Instead of hearing an outward voice, something apart from us, we have an inner consciousness of His abiding presence. This is how we know and recognize the Lord's voice.

The Lord's voice is like an inner infusion and supply

The Lord's voice under the new covenant comes as an inner infusion and supply. Galatians 3:21 says, "Is the law then against the promises of God? Certainly not! *For if there had been a law given which could have given life,* truly righteousness would have been by the law." God's voice under the old covenant was correct and proper in itself, but as an outward law it could not give life. It could not infuse and supply life. It could only tell you what to do. No doubt, the law given by Moses accurately defined our condition, but it could not supply life to carry it out. But John 1:17 says, "For the law was given through Moses, but grace and truth [or, reality] came through Jesus Christ." Grace and reality coming through

Jesus Christ is different from an outward law being handed to us. Grace and reality is the Lord Himself in person coming to us to infuse His very life into our being.

The law was *given* but grace *came*. There is a big difference. For example, I can communicate with you in two ways. I can send you a letter or I can come in person to communicate with you. The law given by Moses is like receiving a communication by letter, but grace and reality coming through Jesus Christ is receiving a communication from Christ Himself. When He comes in person, we receive direct infusion and supply. This supply is the new covenant way God speaks to us. His speaking to us is His simultaneous supply into us. Jesus said in John 6:63, "It is the Spirit who gives life; the flesh profits nothing. *The words that I speak to you are spirit, and they are life*." Thus His speaking means infusion and inner supply.

Furthermore, this speaking is not merely an intermittent or sporadic speaking but a constant supply of life in our being. For example, we may experience an inner infusion of love toward our relatives to pray for their salvation. The love we feel for them is God's way of speaking to us about them. God did not come and outwardly tell us to love our relatives and pray for them. He does not do it that way. Rather, He wells up within us with compassion and burden. The compassion and burden *are* the Lord's voice, because His voice comes with the infusion and supply of what He wants us to do. As we learn to read the feelings within our heart, we are learning to hear the Lord's voice.

Often His voice comes like a little seed planted within our hearts in the form of a thought or burden. If we would pay more attention to those burdens and fan them by prayer, we would discover the voice of God in our daily life in an increasing way. However, if we consider His speaking as merely an objective, outward voice, we may miss the hundreds of times God desires to subjectively and inwardly fulfill something within us.

Paul refers to this inward teaching in 1 Thessalonians 4:9: "But concerning brotherly love you have no need that I should write to you, for you yourselves are taught by God to love one another." The phrase "taught by God" is a compound word in Greek that literally means God-taught *(theodidaktos / θεοδίδακτος).* In other words, we are intuitively God-taught to love one another. According to 1 Thessalonians 4:8 this inward God-kind of teaching is coming from a present and continuous supply of the Holy Spirit.

There is within us a speaking which is teaching us about our relationships with one another. However, the teaching comes in the form of an infusion of the Holy Spirit, rather than in the form of an outward demand. We are all God-taught. This indicates that we have His voice speaking in us about loving one another. John 6:45 says, "they shall *all* be taught by God," and Hebrews 8:11 indicates that these taught ones include the least to the greatest of the saints. This tells us that we all have His voice and we all can experience the infusion and supply of His voice and speaking.

The Lord's voice is like an inner inclination

The Lord's voice infuses and supplies us with love for Him,

godly desires, willingness to obey Him, and the ability to go along with Him. This reveals that His voice is like an inner inclination in our being. That is, He puts His inclinations into us. This is the nature of His speaking. It is not hearing an audible voice; neither is it waiting for a vision; nor is it reading some words that appear before our eyes in a ticker-tape fashion. Rather, the normal voice of the Son speaking in us comes as a supplied feeling of life written into our consciousness. This feeling is an inner inclination or tendency. It may even be considered as an inner bias or disposition. It is the bent and leaning of our mind, emotion, and will. For example, there may be an inclination or desire within you to spend more time with the Lord. You have a leaning in that direction. It is not an overpowering feeling; nevertheless you seem to be bent in the direction of desiring to spend more time with the Lord in your daily life. That inclination is the voice of the Son of God. He is not speaking audibly in your ears, but He is speaking in your inner consciousness by an infused tendency. The tendency carries with it a fresh supply of grace. Thus, whenever you go along with that tendency and obey it, you discover that the bountiful supply of the Spirit of Jesus Christ is present there with you, backing up that tendency with fresh and available grace.

The apostle Paul mentions this inner inclination in Romans 8:5-6: [5] "For those who live according to the flesh set their minds on the things of the flesh, but those who live according to the Spirit, the things of the Spirit. [6] For to be carnally minded is death, but to be spiritually minded is life and peace." To be carnally minded or spiritually minded is to be inwardly inclined. Many translations have attempted to capture this thought in different ways. *The American Standard Version* translates verse 6, "For the *mind* of the flesh is death; but the *mind* of the Spirit is life and peace." *The Concordant Literal New Testament* translates it, "For the *disposition* of the flesh is death, yet the *disposition* of the spirit is life and peace." *The Emphasized Bible* by Rotherham translates the same verse, "For *what is preferred by* the flesh is death, whereas *what is preferred by* the spirit is life and peace." All of these translations attempt to capture the depth of the Greek word *phronema* (φρόνημα) used here by Paul.

This New Testament word *phronema*, according to the Greek lexicons, means the *bent or direction of the mind, emotions, and will.* In other words, it refers to the inclination of all the faculties of our inner being. Romans 8:6 tells us that the very source of this bent and inclination toward life and peace is the Spirit. It is the Spirit that produces a Spirit-inclined disposition in us that registers the consciousness of "life and peace." In fact, this is one of the major things the Spirit accomplishes in us — inclining our inner being toward the things of God.

When we experience inclinations toward God and the things of God, it causes us to worship Him because we realize that the very thing He is inclining us toward, He Himself does. It is all grace! For example, He wants us to love Him, so He Himself imparts into us the love whereby we can love Him. We discover that the love of God is something poured out in our hearts through the Holy Spirit (Rom. 5:5). Another inclination that we discover is a desire to share Christ with others. We gradually begin to realize that the inclination itself *is* the Lord's voice in us prompting us to preach the gospel. There are also times when we wake up in the morning with a few words of a hymn or spiritual song. We are then inclined to go to our hymnal to find the rest of the words of that song. When we do, we are face-to-face with God's specific words or speaking to us for that day. How many times have you been inwardly directed to a devotional book, such as *Daily Light,* only to find the word, the line, or the verse that met your need at that moment?

To hear the sweet sound of the Lord's voice in our daily life, we need to look for and follow the Spirit-produced inclinations. Following these inclinations will issue in the sense of life and peace within. Again, under the new covenant His speaking does not normally come to us as an audible voice. Rather, it comes in the line of a verse, in the words of a song, in the fellowship with another member of the Body, in a message we heard from the Word, or in the growing burden we feel in our hearts. As we open ourselves to live out of the source of the Spirit (Rom. 8:4-5), we will increasingly be made aware of our heart's inclinations (Rom. 8:6). It is in those inclinations that we will find the Lord's voice for our daily life.

10

Compatibility with the Lord's Voice

"We can always know whether we are hearkening to God's voice by whether we have joy or not; if there is no joy, we are not hearkening. Hearkening to the voice of God will produce the joy that Jesus had. 'That My joy may be in you, and that your joy may be fulfilled.' A life of intimacy with God is characterized by joy."

– Oswald Chambers

The Lord's voice and the Lord's life

To properly understand the nature of the Lord's *voice* in us, it is necessary to identify it with the Lord's *life* in us. Indeed, the Lord's indwelling life is *the manner of His voice* speaking in us. The Lord, who is declared to be the Word, the *logos*, in John 1:1, is simultaneously described in verse 4 by the words, "In Him was life, and the life was the light of men." The Lord Jesus as the Word is the One who *is* life and *gives* life. It is this life, which has entered into us through regeneration, that becomes His speaking in us. In experience His voice and His life are virtually the same thing. It is His life that speaks and talks in us all day long. Thus, hearing the Lord's voice and obeying it is the same as being compatible with His life.

The Lord's voice can be described as a life-voice. John 5:25-26 clearly reveals this: [25] "Most assuredly, I say to you, the hour is coming, and now is, when the dead will hear the voice of the Son of God; and those who hear will live. [26] For as the Father has life in Himself, so He has granted the Son to have life in Himself." Hebrews 1:1-2 also declares, [1] "God, who at various times and in different ways spoke in time past to the fathers by the prophets, [2] has in these last days spoken to us in His Son."

Understanding life-consciousness

To understand the Lord's voice as a life-voice, we must understand the main characteristic of the Lord's life in us. This characteristic is revealed in Romans 8:10 which says, "And if Christ is in you, the body is dead because of sin, but the spirit is life because of righteousness" (cf. Col. 3:4). First, Christ, who is our life, is not in us merely in a general way, but He is in us in a specific way. Indeed, He is dwelling and living in our spirit. It is our human spirit that has become the residence of the Lord's life. Second, with the Lord's life in us, there is the corresponding consciousness that belongs to that life. Every kind of life has a life-consciousness. This is true about the nature of animal life and human life as well as the divine life. Every life has its own kind of consciousness. We may say that the consciousness is the inherent voice of the life. The consciousness of life is the intrinsic speaking of that life.

Consciousness, in relation to life, means having an awareness of something, a recognition or a perception of something.

It means to come to know something experientially. Any particular kind of life brings with it its own kind of awareness. For example, in a cat's life we can observe cat-consciousness. Cat life simply brings with it a consciousness and an awareness that is unique to that life. Kittens especially have a vivid imagination. The kind of life they have gives them the kind of consciousness that causes them to flit and dart around as though something was attacking them. This consciousness is due to their cat life. We observe this consciousness in any kind of animal, whether it be a dog, a bird, or a fish. Its particular kind of life gives it a corresponding consciousness that, in turn, expresses itself in some kind of animal behavior. The principle is very clear — with every kind of life, there is a consciousness that goes with that life.

When relating this principle of life-consciousness to human life, there are two main aspects to consider. First, in relation to the physical life in our bodies, we have the normal physical senses of seeing, hearing, smelling, tasting, and touching or feeling. These specific senses have their source in the various organs of our physical life — our eyes, ears, nose, mouth, and our entire body with its inherent ability to touch or feel. For example, because our body can feel a cold temperature, that very feeling is a form of speaking to us. In other words, we do not need to read a sign telling us, "You're cold." Rather, we feel cold, and the feeling itself of being cold is the voice of physical life speaking to us to put on a jacket. Thus, we may say that physical life with its senses has its own unique consciousness. Each consciousness coming from physical life is the voice of physical life speaking to our body. We have often heard such remarks as, "My stomach is telling me I am hungry." What is this, but the recognition that physical life with its physical consciousness does communicate to us.

Second, when considering human life, we must also observe our psychological life. Psychological life in the Bible is called soul-life, from the Greek word *psuche* (ψυχή). Everyone has soul-life. The soul can be identified in many verses in the Bible as that faculty that includes the mind, the emotions, and the will. Because we have a soul, we have the consciousness of soul-life — we think with our intellect, or mind; we feel with our emotion; and we choose with our will, or volition. For example, we can get embarrassed and become self-conscious. We can think thoughts that make us either depressed or happy. In other words, because we have soul-life we experience the consciousness that comes with that kind of life. Our psychological life definitely has its own kind of consciousness. Surely, we can recognize that not only does our psychological life have its consciousness, but that consciousness *is* its voice communicating to us.

Furthermore, an additional part of our psychological life is our conscience. Our conscience is a deeper inner consciousness. We all have this in common due to possessing psychological life. Who can deny that they have the voice of conscience? The Greek word for conscience is *suneidesis* (συνείδησις). This compound word is composed of the preposition "with" and a root word meaning "to know." Thus, by analyzing *conscience* etymologically, we have a clear definition of the word — to know with. Conscience means a "knowing with" or an "inner consciousness." This knowing comes from psychological life.

In the same way, when the divine life enters into us, it comes into us with a definite consciousness. In fact, because the life of God is the highest form of life, it has the highest consciousness. God's life is exceedingly rich in consciousness and feeling. If animal life and human life have consciousness, how much more does the divine life! Because the divine life is a Person in us and not merely an impersonal substance, we begin to experience the rich feelings of God. His love, His joy, His peace, and His compassions stir us from deep within. The apostle Paul clearly depicts these stirrings in Philippians 1:8: "For God is my witness, how greatly I long for you all in the inward parts of Jesus Christ." With Paul those "inward parts of Jesus Christ" were the compassions and affections of Christ that he experienced as a life-consciousness within him. Paul was indwelt with Christ as his life (Col. 3:4), and in his own personal experience he knew the rich feelings of Christ that came from His indwelling life.

Not only did Paul have this life-consciousness, but every born-again believer has such a consciousness as well. Romans 8:10 declares, "And if Christ is in you . . . the spirit is life" (ASV). First Corinthians 15:45 says, "The last Adam [Christ] became a life-giving Spirit"; and 1 Corinthians 6:17 says, "But he who is joined to the Lord is one spirit with Him." This means that Christ as the life-giving Spirit now dwells in our regenerated human spirit, making our spirit life. Thus, our spirit is life because Christ, the life-giver, lives there. This helps us to realize the location of the life-consciousness within us. It is in our spirit! Consequently, not only is our spirit life, but our spirit is the source from which every kind of life-consciousness flows into our being (cf. John 7:37-39; 10:10).

We need to make the connection between experiencing the Lord's *life* and hearing the Lord's *voice*. This connection is presented by the Lord Himself in John 10:10 and 16 as well as John 10:27-28: [10] "I have come that they may have *life,* and that they may have it more abundantly.... [16] And other sheep I have which are not of this fold; them also I must bring, and they will hear My *voice;* and there will be one flock and one shepherd.... [27] My sheep hear My *voice,* and I know them, and they follow Me. [28] And I give them eternal *life,* and they shall never perish; neither shall anyone snatch them out of My hand." By these verses we can see *the way* the Lord's voice is experienced by us. It is by the Lord's life that we experience His voice. It is a life-voice!

Compatibility with the Lord's life

As we apprehend how hearing the Lord's voice is interrelated with knowing the Lord's life, it is important to learn compatibility with the Lord's life. Hearing the Lord and being one with His speaking is the same as being compatible with His life. Indeed, following the Lord in our daily life is a matter of always remaining compatible with His life. As regenerated believers we have Another life in us that has another feeling and another consciousness. As we experience His life, we discover different kinds of responses within us that are according to His life. These responses tell us how to remain compatible.

If we do not remain compatible with the Lord's life in any area of our living, we will sense an inward awkwardness and lack. For example, in Colossians 3:15 Paul says, "And let the peace of Christ rule in your hearts, to which also you were called in one Body; and be thankful." If I do not let the peace of Christ make the decision in my heart when I am tempted to engage in argumentative talk, at that moment I am not compatible with the feeling or registration of the Lord's life within me. As a result of not remaining compatible, we feel the effects within ourselves. We may sense that we are at odds with the Lord. Even *we* do not feel quite normal in our demeanor or inward posture.

On those occasions the Lord is not speaking to us with a loudspeaker out of the heavens; rather, He manifests His voice to us by the feeling or registration of His life. The Lord feels a certain way within us, producing either the sense of "life and peace," which tells us that we are compatible with His life, or a sense of "death," which tells us that something in our talking, our attitude, or our behavior does not match the nature of His life within. Romans 8:6 says, "The mind of the flesh is death; but the mind of the Spirit is life and peace" (ASV). In our experience the mind of the flesh is the consciousness of death, and the mind of the Spirit is the consciousness of life and peace. Of course, the more we drink of the Lord as the Spirit day by day, the richer and deeper will be our fellowship with Him, and the richer and deeper will be our sensitivity to the consciousness of His life. This means we will be one of His sheep that are compatible with His life-voice (John 10:27).

The meaning of compatibility

Being compatible with the Lord's voice and life simply means being agreeable with Him on His terms. It means always being harmonious with His registrations of life and peace within us in our daily life. It is by living compatibly with Him that we grow in life, spontaneously being changed and transformed into His image. So not only do we enjoy Him in a general way; but as we enjoy Him we grow rich in the consciousness of that life. We learn to specifically recognize His inner approval or disapproval in our walk. In other words, we seek to make that life happy and satisfied all day long. Whenever that life is not happy and satisfied, we quickly care for it to make it happy again.

As a believer I may know doctrinally that there is "no condemnation to those who are in Christ Jesus" (Rom. 8:1). Yet why do I still feel condemned? Why do I feel "out of sorts" within? If I am not under the law but under grace, then why do I experience discomfort and awkwardness within when I take a certain course of action? These kinds of questions have troubled many believers for years. The answer to these questions is quite simple. Yes, we are positionally "in Christ," and therefore we are justified persons and there is no condemnation. Yet whenever we do things that are not in harmony with the Lord's life, *we feel* the responses and reactions of Christ within our being, because He is, in fact, *"our life"* (Col. 3:4). This is the significance of the phrase in Romans 5:18, "justification of life." It means a justification that issues, or results, in a life-consciousness within us.

God's salvation over us includes not only justification; it also includes regeneration. Justification refers to our secure standing before God based upon the blood of Christ. Regeneration refers to the life of God that we have received into our spirit making us one spirit with the Lord. Justification is positional, whereas regeneration is dispositional. Regeneration is a matter of the divine life entering into us and inwardly guiding us throughout our life. Whenever we pursue a course of action that is not compatible with the Lord's life, our regenerated state causes us to feel bothered. We cannot remain inwardly content, because we are at odds with His life. His life within cannot change its life-consciousness. We are simply incompatible at that point. Our standing has not changed, but our present condition is incompatible. This disturbance of our inward harmony *is* the Lord's voice in us speaking to us to get us back on course with the divine life. He is not condemning us, but rather He is loving us by inwardly steering us back to Himself. Hallelujah!

The basis of compatibility

The basis of our being compatible with the Lord's voice is our life-union with Him in spirit. This union is expressed by the Lord's words in John 14:19: "A little while longer and the world will see Me no more, but you will see Me. Because I live, you will live also." We live because He lives. It is that simple. First Corinthians 6:17 reveals that this union with the Lord is in the realm of our spirit. We are joined to the Lord and are one spirit with Him. This joining is the basis of the Lord's words, "Because I live, you will live also." He lives within us in our spirit, and we live in union with Him. This life-union issues in a life-consciousness. So we can know and experience the very consciousness of the Lord's life within us. It is by this life-consciousness that we learn to be compatible with His life-voice.

This experiential reality is also expressed in John 4:14: "But whoever drinks of the water that I shall give him will never thirst. But the water that I shall give him will become in him a fountain of water springing up into eternal life." When the Lord said, "the water that I shall give him *will become in him a fountain of water*," He was referring to our life-union with Him. When we receive Christ, an "artesian well" is established in the deepest part of our being, in our spirit. When this life-union, or inner well, springs up within us, it produces the consciousness of His life in the many facets of our daily life — from our inner thinking and motives to our outward behavior and deeds. Again, it is this life-consciousness that is the Lord's voice. When we go along with this consciousness, we are being compatible with God.

Ephesians 2:5 says, "even when we were dead in trespasses, [God] made us alive together with Christ (by grace you have been saved)." To be dead in offenses means being a person without feeling, having no proper spiritual consciousness. A dead person can be defined as a person without any consciousness. Apart from regeneration there is no basis or ground to be compatible with the Lord. But when we are born again, we are regenerated with Another life and we are made alive together with Christ. And because we are alive together with Him by a new birth, we possess His life-consciousness within us. It is our being "alive together with Christ" in a life-union that provides the basis for being compatible with the Lord's voice moment by moment.

The anointing and being compatible

Being compatible with the Lord's voice is also described by the apostle John as being taught by the anointing. In 1 John 2:20 and 27 we read, [20] "But you have an anointing from the Holy One, and you know all things.... [27] But the anointing which you have received from Him abides in you, and you do not need that anyone teach you; but as the same anointing teaches you concerning all things, and is true, and is not a lie, and just as it has taught you, you will abide in Him." The word *anointing* is the verbal form of the noun *the Anointed One.* Anointing in Greek is *chrisma* (χρίσμα) and simply refers to the movement and action of the Anointed One, Christ — *Christos* (Χριστός).

John says, "the same anointing teaches you." This means the movement and action of the Lord within us has the ability to communicate to us and teach us. Thus, the way we hear the Lord's voice is by the anointing. This kind of speaking does not come in the form of plain words written on a page. Rather, it is an inner movement of the Anointed One within us. The anointing abides *in* us. This anointing should not be thought of as an extraordinary gift that a few spiritual people possess. The anointing is simply the movement and inner activity of Christ Himself in all His redeemed and regenerated children.

In our daily experience the anointing teaches us by giving us an inner knowing. This teaching is by the life movement and consciousness within us. It is a different kind of teaching from the Old Testament law of letters written on tablets of stone. The anointing is a kind of teaching that comes out of our fellowship with the Lord and our inner sensitivity to Him.

Compatibility in negative experiences

We may liken the teaching of the anointing to our being taught in the physical realm. For example, if we walk into a room in which the temperature is one hundred degrees, the presence of heat teaches us to take off our jacket. There is no need to read a sign that says, "Take off your jacket." The presence of heat automatically teaches us to take it off. It is the *presence* of something that teaches, not a teaching by audible words or outward letters of instruction. We can say that the temperature itself teaches us with the voice of a "felt presence." The anointing works in the same way within us. The anointing is the presence of a Person moving within us. Thus, whenever we are taking a certain course of action that is not compatible with the Lord, we sense a bothering or troubling within. We lose our normal inward poise of peace. For instance, you are about to complain to someone because you are right and they are wrong about something they did or did not do. But as you actually launch into your argument, the more you speak, the more there is the presence of "heat." You feel uncomfortable, you feel awkward, you lose your peace, and you yourself sense that what you are saying is not compatible with your insides.

Just as heat teaches you to take off your jacket, so the presence of the anointing teaches you to stop talking in a complaining way. The reason you are unable to keep talking is not because someone is telling you not to talk that way. You cannot talk because *you* have an inward forbidding. You are simply not free and at liberty to speak that way anymore. This kind of experience is the anointing teaching you. The anointing's voice made it clear that your words were not compatible with the Lord. This kind of experience is not an occasion for taking condemning thoughts and accusations about yourself. Rather, it is an occasion for learning to be compatible with the Lord's life in your speaking and attitude.

Compatibility in neutral matters

Learning to be compatible by following the anointing applies not only in negative matters; the anointing is also operating in our lives in the face of neutral matters where sin and the flesh are not involved. Sometimes we are faced with decisions of guidance related to what we should do or where we should go. The apostle Paul bears testimony to this in his own life in 2 Corinthians 2:12-14: [12] "Furthermore, when I came to Troas to preach Christ's gospel, and a door was opened to me by the Lord, [13] I had no rest in my spirit, because I did not find Titus my brother; but taking my leave of them, I departed for Macedonia. [14] Now thanks be to God who always leads us in triumph in Christ, and through us diffuses the fragrance of His knowledge in every place. " Paul had an open door to preach the gospel, but in his spirit he did not find the rest to do so. This means *the lack of rest* in his spirit *was* the Lord's voice indicating to him that to preach the gospel in Troas at that juncture was not compatible with the Lord's mind.

Luke records a similar experience of Paul's in Acts 16:6-7, [6]"Now when they had gone through Phrygia and the region of Galatia, they were forbidden by the Holy Spirit to preach the word in Asia. [7]After they had come to Mysia, they tried to go into Bithynia, but the Spirit of Jesus did not permit them." In both instances, the anointing of the Spirit spoke in a way to "forbid" and "not permit" as they were proceeding to preach the Word. No doubt, Paul's fellowship with the Lord was rich and deep, and his inward parts were sensitive to hear the Lord's voice manifesting itself not by outward words but by an inward restraint.

Intimacy and compatibility

To understand what it means to live a life of compatibility with the Lord, we need to consider the example of the Lord's human living. What we see in the Lord's relationship with the Father is that His compatibility with the Father came out of His intimacy with the Father. John 1:18 reveals that the only begotten Son is "into the bosom of the Father." This shows His intimate fellowship with the Father. John 15:9-10 indicates that He was abiding in the Father's love. It was out of this kind of love-intimacy that He lived a life of complete compatibility with the Father's life and will.

The Lord's example reveals the principle by which we can live day by day being compatible with His voice. It is simple. Compatibility with the divine life comes by cultivating a life of intimacy. We all recognize that this is true in the marriage life. How is a wife compatible with her husband? How does she live to please her husband? The compatibility of a wife with her husband is dependent upon her intimacy with her husband. Her intimacy with her husband creates and nurtures the desire to please him.

The Holy Spirit's terms in the New Testament for compatibility are "pleasing" and "well pleasing." John 8:28-29 says, [28] "Then Jesus said to them, When you lift up the Son of Man, then you will know that I am He, and that I do nothing of Myself; but as My Father taught Me, I speak these things. [29] And He who sent Me is with Me. The Father has not left Me alone, for I always do those things that *please* Him." In other words, the reason for His compatibility with the Father was that He heard the Father's voice because of His life of intimacy with the Father. He was sensitive to what the Father *taught* Him, not only because the Father was with Him all the time, but because He was always abiding in the Father's love. This was the reason there was such a constant supply coming from the Lord. He lived in the Father and was always doing that which was compatible with the Father.

According to the prophecy about the Lord's life in Isaiah 50:4-5, the Father woke Him morning by morning and opened His ear to hear His voice. Then we observe in the Gospels the way He lived His life from morning to night. He always did the things that pleased the Father — where He went, those He saw, those He prayed for, those He related to. His intimacy with the Father was the factor that supplied the ability to live a life compatible with the Father.

By observing the Lord's life of intimacy and compatibility with the Father, we discover the nature of the life that is now dwelling in us. It is a life that thrives on intimacy with the Father (Gal. 4:6; Rom. 8:15). It is a life that always desires to prove, by testing, what is well pleasing to the Lord (cf. Eph. 5:10). It is a life that knows compatibility with the Father's life-voice in all the details of daily life (Eph. 4:20-21). Now this life is living in us. Hallelujah!

May the Lord grant to us multiplied grace in our spirit, so that the love of God, the grace of Christ, and the fellowship of the Holy Spirit would be our daily portion (2 Cor. 13:14). As we inwardly merge with the intimacy in the Triune God, we will not only abide in His love, but we will also develop a finer and more delicate sensitivity to the consciousness of life within us. It is by the love of God and the grace of Christ flowing in the fellowship of the Holy Spirit that we can be a person who is compatible with the Lord's voice. Amen!

11

The Law of Life and the Lord's Voice

"There is a dialogue ever in process between the Good Shepherd and His own. He not only calls them by name as He leads them forth, but He talks to them, encouraging, soothing, communing with them about His purposes, explaining His reasons, indicting His commands. Holy souls become aware of impressions which are made on them from time to time, promptings, inspirations, largely through the words of Scripture, and sometimes otherwise, which they recognize as the Shepherd's voice. That voice ever calls to self-sacrifice, fellowship, purity, and is different to all other voices."

– *F. B. Meyer*

Understanding the law of life

We have observed that with every kind of life there is a corresponding consciousness that is intrinsically part of that life. The presence of life *is* the presence of consciousness. The consciousness of any form of life may also be considered as an inherent law of that life. Thus, the inherent law requires it to behave in a particular way. For example, the law of the cat life requires it to chase mice. The law of the dog life requires it to bark. The law of the bird life requires it to fly.

We can see that with every kind of life there is a law that *requires* and even *demands* it to behave according to the law of its life.

With our physical life there is also a law. For example, the law of our physical life requires us to sleep. The requirement to sleep is built into our physical life. There is no need to go to school to learn how to sleep. Sleep is not something taught. Sleep is a requirement and demand of physical life. Thus, because we have physical life, inherently and automatically we require sleep.

By these examples we can see that there is a fixed principle related to life: with every kind of life there is a law of that life requiring it to behave in a certain way. Dogs barking, cats chasing mice, human beings needing sleep, stomachs feeling hungry, are simply the requirements of these respective lives. These requirements are not outward legalities or something imposed from without; rather, they are inherent demands from within the life — they make up the law of that life.

To understand the Lord's voice in us, it is necessary to understand the law of His indwelling life. Under the new covenant God's speaking is in His Son (Heb. 1:2). The Son comes into us by imparting His life into us. And He speaks by the vitality and force of the Spirit giving us life and inclining our very being in the way He wants us to go (Ezek. 36:26-27). The Lord's speaking is not normally of the nature of an audible voice. Rather, the nature of the Lord's voice is a life-voice (John 10:27-28). In our experience the Lord's voice is synonymous with the law and requirements of the Lord's life.

Thus, we need to understand the law of the Spirit of life that the apostle Paul speaks of in Romans 8:2.

The basic principle in knowing and discerning the Lord's life is that we become progressively acquainted with *the requirement of that life*. Through regeneration Christ now lives in us as *our* life (Col. 3:4). On one hand, since His life is His life, it is going to react and behave according to its own nature. On the other hand, since His life is also *our life,* we are going to experience the reactions of that life, especially when we go against its nature. To live incompatibly with the Lord's life is to live a frustrated and miserable Christian life. We cannot change the way His life reacts. His life, reacting from within our spirit (Rom. 8:10), is like a compass that always points in one direction. Whatever way you turn the compass, the arrow points north. Similarly, regardless of how we may reason and argue with the Lord's life, we cannot change its nature. It is eternally destined to react and behave according to the life that is in Christ Jesus. Thus, to live compatibly with His life is to go along with the law of that life.

It is important at this juncture to point out the difference between outward demand and inward requirement. There is a difference. The former is related to the letter of the law and brings in bondage; the latter is related to the Spirit of life that brings in freedom. Outward demand is accompanied with condemnation, but the inward law of life is accompanied with grace and life-supply. When you are controlled by outward demand, as in Romans 7, you end in failure. But when you are controlled by the law of life, you experience God's inner operation, as in Romans 8 and Philippians 2:12-13.

The requirement of life is what Romans 8:2 identifies as *the law* of the Spirit of life in Christ Jesus. The law of gravity requires objects to be pulled downward. This law always behaves in this particular way. In the same way, the life of Christ within us requires that it behave in a certain way. This is why the apostle Paul speaks of "*the law* of the Spirit of life in Christ Jesus." It is because the law of the Spirit of life *is* the law inherent in the divine life. The law of life is simply the requirement of that life. In other words, when the divine life enters into our being, it brings with it its own requirements. Paul says in Romans 8:4, "that the righteous requirement of the law might be fulfilled in us who do not walk according to the flesh but according to spirit." Thus, when we walk according to spirit something is fulfilled in us. It is not fulfilled *by* us, but *in* us. The righteous requirement of the law is now fulfilled in Christ. Christ did not come to destroy the law or the prophets; He came to fulfill (cf. Matt. 5:17). He not only fulfilled the law, but He uplifted the law of God to its true source — the life of God.

According to the Lord's teaching in Matthew 5—7, the law of letters is superseded by the law of life. He revealed that what God was after was not mere outward righteousness and performance, but an inward life that touches our lives at the level of motive, lust, reaction, and disposition. It is this deeper life-level that the Lord came to fulfill in us. Therefore, the righteous requirement of the law that is fulfilled in us is none other than the life of the Person living and operating in us. For example, to live a life of not looking upon a woman to lust after her is not merely an outward demand of the law. It is the inner requirement of the life of Christ within (Matt. 5:27-30). His life demands holiness and purity because that is its nature. He is not merely giving us an outward law, but He is describing the nature of His life within. For this reason, when we indulge our lusts we sense inward turmoil and conflict. This is the effect of being incompatible with the law of His life.

In the same way, if we do not go along with the requirement of sleep, our outward, physical life feels the effect. Physical life will automatically feel the effects of sleep loss. Not being compatible with the law of our physical life that requires sleep will surely weaken and fatigue us. Similarly, as believers we have "the life of God" dwelling within us (Eph. 4:18; Rom. 8:9-11). Inherent in the life are its requirements. Whenever we go against those requirements, we feel the effects upon our inner life. Understanding the principle of the law of life is crucial to properly discern the Lord's speaking and voice in us. His voice is a life-voice. Thus, to hear His voice is to learn to be compatible with the law of His life.

The Word defines the life within us

To better know and understand the law of the Spirit of life in our lives, we need to read the Bible. The Word of God defines for us the specific areas related to the requirement of life. In fact, we may consider the New Testament letters as a record of the life of God practically lived out in the lives of the saints. Thus, if we are not clear about what the Lord is doing in us according to our own consciousness of life, we can read the explanation and definition of life in the Word and become clearer about our own inner registrations. For example, in Ephesians 4:17-19, the apostle Paul describes how the ungodly world is "alienated from *the life of God*." He then contrasts this with the believers by saying in verses 20 and 21, [20] "But you have not so learned Christ, [21] if indeed you have heard Him and have been taught by Him, as the truth is in Jesus." To learn Christ, according to these verses, is to learn that the inner law of His life is a requirement to put off the old manner of life with its lusts and deceit (v.22). Thus, when we are tempted to go back to our old life of sin, we will discover that there is something *constant and unchanging* in our being. That something is *His life* with its demand and requirement to deal with our old manner of life. Although we may not quickly heed the inward prodding of life to put off an old habit or indulgence, every time we go to the Bible we will be faced with verse after verse that in one way or another defines the divine life's requirement to deal with our old manner of life. Thus, the outward, written Word (*logos* / λόγος) will always confirm the inward, spoken word (*rhema* / ῥῆμα), and vice versa.

In our Christian life we need to learn to live compatibly with the law or requirement of the divine life. If that requirement or demand is vague to us, God has given us His Word to define and describe it. In other words, there has already been a laboratory experience of the divine life in the apostles' lives, and the record has been preserved for us in their writings. For example, within the pages of the New Testament, Paul wrote and even admonished saints in a certain way. This is because he was speaking according to the knowledge he had of the requirements of the divine life. He knew that the life in him was the same life dwelling in all the saints, having the same kind of requirements. Thus, he wrote to them according to his knowledge and experience of that life. He was able to address their problems in a way that led them to know the Lord as life, rather than to merely change their outward behavior.

Thank God that the Word of God explains and defines the life of God within us. We become increasingly clear about the requirement of the divine life in our daily living by prayerfully reading the Word. Hebrews 4:12 tells us, "For the word of God is living and powerful, and sharper than any two-edged sword, piercing even to the division of soul and spirit, and of joints and marrow, and is a discerner of the thoughts and intents of the heart." If we are confused and our feelings are undefined, the Word will divide our soul and spirit and bring in the clarity that we need to better correspond with His life. The closer we stay to the Word, the clearer we will be concerning the Lord's life-voice within us.

Examples of the requirement of life

An example of the requirement of life operating in our life is found in Colossians 3:3-5: [3]"For you died, and your life is hidden with Christ in God. [4] When Christ who is our life appears, then you also will appear with Him in glory. [5] Therefore put to death your members which are on the earth: fornication, uncleanness, passion, evil desire, and covetousness, which is idolatry." From verses 3 and 4 we know assuredly that Christ is our life. Then in verse 5 Paul specifically defines the requirement of that life by speaking in the imperative mood. He says, "Therefore put to death your members which are on the earth." Paul speaks in the imperative mood when he is dealing with something that he knows is an inner requirement of life. When Paul speaks in the imperative, "Put to death," he is not doing so as a law-giver under the old covenant, but as a life-identifier under the new covenant.

To speak in the imperative mood (the mood of command or entreaty) in the New Testament is always based upon facts that already exist in the indicative mood (the mood of fact). The requirements of life are facts that exist in us because of our spirit-union with the Lord (1 Cor. 6:17). Thus, in Colossians 3:3 Paul says, "You died" and "Your life is hidden with Christ in God." Our being dead and our life being hidden are both facts expressed in the indicative mood. This kind of speaking identifies the facts that are true of every believer's inner life. Then Paul changes to the imperative mood by saying in verse 5, "Therefore put to death your members which are on the earth." In moving from the indicative to the imperative mood, Paul does not leave the realm of the spirit and life. Rather, he affirms *what is true* in the Spirit (indicative) and equally affirms *what is required* by the Spirit (imperative).

This is what we mean by the requirement of life or the demand of life. It is simply knowing that the Lord's voice in us will always be according to the nature of His life. If the nature of His life is one that died to sin and to the old man (Rom. 6:2-11 uses over 10 indicatives), then the requirement of His life in us will always be an inner imperative (Rom. 6:12-

13 uses 2 imperatives). Thus, Paul says, "*Therefore do not let sin reign* in your mortal body," and "*Present yourselves* to God as being alive from the dead." In other words, the requirement or imperative of life demands that we deal with sin reigning in our lives and that we live a life wholly given to the Lord. This kind of demand is not an outward demand of the law on our flesh; rather, it is an inward demand originating from the life in our spirit.

In experience, this inward demand is like an inward necessity. It is the necessity of life. Once the life of God indwells us, it is necessary for that life to feel at home in every part of our being. Indeed, it yearns for compatibility (James 4:5). It is like a fish that finds its compatibility in the element of water. If we go along with the life-requirements, then our inner being will be full of peace and joy. But if we go against them, we will suffer the consequences of not being compatible with the life of God within. If we have heard His life-voice as an inner imperative for us to break with sin, and we respond to that voice in obedience, we will discover the life-supply of the Spirit coming to us to strengthen us to carry out the obedience.

The requirement to deal with our moral life

In Colossians 3, the requirement of life is to deal with our moral life. Things such as fornication, uncleanness, passion, evil desire, and greediness are specifically mentioned by Paul. All of these things are totally incompatible with the Lord's indwelling life. Thus, the life within will always move us to deal with these things in our lives. The life requirement will never change to become more tolerant toward fornication and uncleanness. It will constantly demand that we deal with these things by the Spirit. How we interact with the requirement of life will issue either in the sense of death or in the sense of life. Paul states this fact in Romans 8:13: "For if you live according to the flesh you will die; but if by the Spirit you put to death the deeds of the body, you will live."

Just as much as our body demands sleep, the life of God in us demands that we stay far away from anything immoral (1 Cor. 6:18). Any inordinate relationship, any pornographic material, anything suggestive on the television, any loose or coarse talking and joking — any provision we make to fulfill the lust of the flesh — must be crucified if we are to live compatibly with the requirement of His life-voice (Rom. 13:14; Gal 5:24-25). If we want to be inwardly bright and shining, if we want to be full of life, full of desires for God, and full of love for the church life and God's eternal purpose, then we need to be strict with the requirement of life. This means we are governed inwardly to always do the things that please Christ *our life*. Whenever we go along with His requirements in our moral life, there is always a supply of grace and refreshment to our inner man. God is happy and we are happy!

The requirement of life to prove what is well pleasing to the Lord

When Paul spoke the words in Ephesians 5:10, "Proving what is well pleasing to the Lord," he was appealing to the saints to care for the requirement of their inner life. In the context of Ephesians 5, the requirement of life is related to dealings with the Lord over our social life, our community life, our friends and associates. This is confirmed in verses 11-12: [11] "And have no fellowship with the unfruitful works of darkness, but rather expose them. [12] For it is shameful even to speak of those things which are done by them in secret." Thus, according to these verses, there is in our experience a proving of what is well pleasing to the Lord, and this proving has to do with what we allow ourselves to participate in.

The apostle Peter spoke in the same way to the saints in 1 Peter 4:1-4: [1] "For he who has suffered in the flesh has ceased from sin, [2] that he no longer should live the rest of his time in the flesh for the lusts of men, but for the will of God. [3] For we have spent enough of our past lifetime in doing the will of the Gentiles — when we walked in licentiousness, lusts, drunkenness, revelries, drinking parties, and abominable idolatries. [4] In regard to these, they think it strange that you do not run with them in the same flood of dissipation, speaking evil of you." The word "they" in verse 4 refers to the old social crowd. They think it is strange that you do not run with them anymore into the same sinful and fleshly life.

The requirement of life will operate in us to prove or test what kind of social life matches the Lord's life within us. Also, the fact that the word "proving" in Ephesians 5:10 is in the present tense indicates that learning to be compatible with the Lord's life-voice is a day-by-day matter. It may also imply that we will pass through some experiences in which we will learn the requirement of life by trial and error, that is, by the negative effect the wrong associations have upon us. It is like going down a dead-end street many times and discovering by experience that it is a dead end. After a few times of trial and error, the effect will be that we will no longer go down that dead-end street, because we proved by experience that it is a dead end.

In the same way, when we touch the life of God, there is a law in that life to have a new community life and a new social life. This new social life is a life in "the new man" (Col. 3:10), which is the church, the Body of Christ. It is a life *in* the Body, *for* the Body, and *with* the Body. The life in us is a life with a Body-consciousness in it. Thus, the law in that life is to adjust our living so that it is well pleasing to the Lord. That is why participating in the unfruitful works of darkness will always end, spiritually speaking, on a dead-end street. The effect upon us is death. Again, it works like our physical life. When I am not going along with the demand of sleep, I am tired and weak; my physical life feels the effects. A law is in operation —the law of physical life that requires sleep. In the same way, the life of God requires light and not darkness. Stay in the light, live in the light, and fellowship in the light. By caring for and heeding this law of life, we will prove what is well pleasing to the Lord right within ourselves.

The law of life and being God-taught

In 1 Thessalonians 4:9 we see another example of the law of life operating automatically within us. In this verse Paul says, "But concerning brotherly love you have no need that I should write to you, for you yourselves are taught by God to love one another." Here Paul directly appealed to what he knew already existed within the saints. Because the divine life was dwelling in them, he could simply identify the divine activity in their inner being. They were taught by God. The phrase "taught by God" in the original Greek is actually a compound word and is better translated "God-taught" *theodidaktos* (θεοδίδακτος). It is a compound word similar to what is found in 2 Timothy 3:16, "All Scripture is God-breathed" *theopneustos* (θεόπνευστος). "God-breathed" describes the inner nature of the Bible.

To be God-taught refers to being taught in our spirit, or more specifically, in the intuition of our spirit. The intuition of our spirit is an immediate sensitivity and perception that originates from Christ being our life in spirit (Col. 3:4; Rom. 8:10). Thus, to be God-taught to love one another is simply to learn to recognize God's love resident within us. This love has not only been poured out in our hearts through the Holy Spirit, but it spontaneously reacts within us as a deep inner affection toward the needs of others (Rom. 5:5 and 1 John 3:17). First John 3:14 says, "We know that we have passed from death to life, because we love the brethren. He who does not love his brother abides in death." Thus, we can see that loving one another is a requirement of the divine life.

Again, we can use the example of our physical body. We are, so to speak, *body-taught* to eat and sleep. Eating and sleeping are not legalities for us to learn or keep, but are demands which originate from and belong to the physical life in our bodies. Thus, we are body-taught to eat and sleep. Our body speaks to us by the demand and requirement of its life.

In the same way, the Lord's speaking in us is by the demand and requirement of His life. That life will require us to deal with the selfishness that might cause us to shut up our affections toward the needy. Thus, the more we experience His life flowing out of our spirit, the more we will be God-taught about so many things in our daily life (John 4:14; Rom. 8:5). We will increasingly hear His life-voice.

The requirement of life and "within the law of Christ"

When Paul was speaking to the believers in Corinth about his relationship to the law, he made a revealing statement that has become a window into his inner life. In 1 Corinthians 9:20-21 he says, [20]"To the Jews I became as a Jew, in order to win Jews; to those under the law I became as one under the law—though not being myself under the law—that I might win those under the law. [21] To those outside the law I became as one outside the law—not being without law toward God but *under [or, within] the law of Christ*—that I might win those outside the law" (RSV).

In verse 21, Paul's statements indicate that he did not want to risk being misunderstood about his relationship to the law of God. He carefully qualifies himself when he talks about being without law. He did not want to give the impression in his speaking that he was a lawless person. Perhaps some would think that since believers are under grace and not under law, they have a license to live loosely and even to sin without compunction (Rom. 6:15). This kind of thinking and practice is known as antinomianism (against law), and has surfaced in the history of the church during the periods when the grace of God was being strongly revealed and proclaimed. This was especially a problem at the time of the Reformation under Luther and also with the evangelical awakening under Wesley and Whitefield.

When Paul says that he was not without law to God but *under* or *within the law of Christ*, he was referring to the requirement of the law of life within his being. He was saying in effect, "I am regulated and controlled by a higher law — the law written by the Spirit into my mind and on my heart under the new covenant (Heb. 8:10-11; 2 Cor. 3:3, 6). It is the law of the Spirit of life in Christ Jesus that set me free from the law of sin and death (Rom. 8:2). It is the inner ruling of what the apostle Paul calls "the righteous requirement of the law," and it is being fulfilled *in* me as I live and walk according to spirit (Rom. 8:4). It is the reality of the uplifted law of God revealed in the Sermon on the Mount. This uplifted law was not destroyed but fulfilled in Christ and is now being reproduced in me by His indwelling life (Matt. 5:17; Rom. 7:4, 6).

To be "under the law of Christ" simply means "within law *in relation to* Christ." That is, in our union and fellowship with the Lord's life, we automatically come under the law of that life. In experience this law will manifest itself as an ethical imperative in our daily affairs. We discover that in the Lord's life there is a higher principle and a higher law. In our living, this higher law issues in going the second mile and turning the other cheek — dealing not merely with our actions, but with our reactions.

To be *under* or *within the law of Christ* means living by the law of life. The Lord's speaking by these life-impulses is finer and more exacting than the outward law. He does not give one inch to the mind of our flesh with its imaginations and independent thinking. He does not give us any space to entertain bitterness toward anyone. He does not allow any room for our tongue to gossip. Rather, the life in us requires that we enter into its very nature of divine love and forgiveness. So we are brought to another level. The life within us requires us to talk on the higher plane of giving grace and building up (Eph. 4:29-30).

The law of life is the same as the consciousness of life or the sense of life. We are not going to change the life of God within us. The life requires actions and reactions that are compatible with its nature. We may ignore or refuse to pay attention to the voice of these life-demands for a long period of time, but eventually we will realize that the requirement of His voice does not change and will not change. He will bring us back to the place from where we have fallen (Rev. 2:5, 7). We will hear Him speaking to us once again, "He who has an ear, let him hear what the Spirit says . . ." May the Lord grant us much grace to recognize more quickly and more regularly His life-voice as we learn to enjoy Him and follow Him in the details of our daily life.

The law of life and our conscience

In understanding the law of life in our experience, we need to see how it is related to our conscience. Learning to follow the voice of conscience is the proper way for a believer to learn to hear the Lord's life-voice within. This is because our conscience is interrelated with our regenerated spirit (cf. Rom. 9:1 with 8:16). So if our conscience is not clear, our spirit cannot properly function and be released. This is a basic principle in our Christian life.

Our conscience may be regarded as the leading function of our spirit. In his own life, Paul maintained the principle of keeping a clear conscience. He testifies in Acts 24:15-16: [15]"I have hope in God, which they themselves also accept, that there will be a resurrection of the dead, both of the just and the unjust. [16]This being so, I myself always strive to have a conscience without offense toward God and men." Paul exercised himself to keep his conscience clear so that his relationship with the Lord would be up to date and also so that he would be ready for the judgment seat of Christ at the resurrection of the righteous. Thus, it is important to have a relationship with the Lord that is governed by the voice of conscience.

The voice of conscience is God's appointed means for man to learn to be inwardly regulated (Rom. 2:14-15). The conscience approves or disapproves our actions and words (Rom. 13:4-7). The basic lesson of learning to live by the Lord's voice in us is to learn to listen to the voice of our own conscience (cf. 2 Tim. 1:3 with Rom. 1:9). If we do not practice this, how could we discern the requirement of the Lord's life in us? Therefore, in our daily life when the Lord is teaching us to hear His voice, the first lessons we learn are to pay attention to the voice of our own conscience. For example,

Paul called upon his conscience as a witness in Romans 9:1 when he was about to make a statement that sounded like a lie (Rom. 9:2-3). Thus, learning to speak the truth with others and learning to communicate accurately, without exaggeration, are all conscience matters that affect our inner life. When we follow the requirement of our conscience by obeying it over matters pertaining to right and wrong, we will be inwardly genuine and exercised to learn the requirement of the Lord's life in other areas related to the intuition of our spirit (2 Cor. 2:12-13).

Experiences of dealing with our conscience may vary from believer to believer according to the kind of knowledge that has been built up within each one. Some knowledge we have received may not be so proper or accurate according to basic truths revealed in Scripture; nevertheless, this knowledge has shaped our conscience a certain way (1 Cor. 8:4-12). The apostle Paul addresses this matter both in 1 Corinthians 8 and Romans 14. In Romans 14:6-9 Paul says, [6]"He who observes the day, observes it to the Lord; and he who does not observe the day, to the Lord he does not observe it. He who eats, eats to the Lord, for he gives God thanks; and he who does not eat, to the Lord he does not eat, and gives God thanks. [7]For none of us lives to himself, and no one dies to himself. [8]For if we live, we live to the Lord; and if we die, we die to the Lord. Therefore, whether we live or die, we are the Lord's. [9]For to this end Christ died and rose and lived again, that He might be Lord of both the dead and the living." These verses reveal that we always need to behave ourselves according to "the present state" of our conscience. In other words, we need to care for whatever requirement or speaking there is in our conscience, even if the knowledge in our conscience is incomplete or inadequate.

In the above verses from Romans 14, Paul gives us some practical examples of various kinds of requirements in a believer's conscience. These examples show how the requirement coming from the voice of conscience is present, even when the conscience is weak because of inadequate knowledge. One person's relationship with the Lord is bound up with his regarding "the day." That is, his conscience is peaceful when he religiously observes a certain day as a special day for the Lord. Another person is peaceful in his relationship with the Lord when he abstains from eating meat. In other words, his having a good conscience to fellowship with the Lord is also bound up with his keeping the requirement of his conscience to refrain from eating meat. Although both of these believers possess inadequate knowledge, they can still live to the Lord and be in the reality of righteousness, peace, and joy in the Holy Spirit (Rom. 14:17).

Paul further explains this spiritual phenomenon in Romans 14:22-23: [22] "Do you have faith? Have it to yourself before God. Happy is he who does not condemn himself in what he approves. [23] But he who doubts is condemned if he eats, because he does not eat from faith; for whatever is not from faith is sin." Thus, if a believer doubts when he eats, due to inadequate knowledge in his conscience, it is better not to eat in that state of heart and mind. This shows that our relationship with the Lord is definitely related to the requirement of our conscience. To be a person living to the Lord we must heed the requirement of conscience.

Learning to recognize and go along with the voice of conscience is the gateway to knowing the Lord's voice in our daily life. As we spend more time in the Word, letting the Bible identify and define the law of life, we will become more sensitive to the Lord's inner speaking in us. Not only so, but as we by faith obey the requirement of life in our moral life, in our personal life, in our attitudes, and in our relationships, we will progressively learn to intimately know the voice of the One who said, "My sheep hear My voice, and I know them, and they follow Me. And I give them eternal life" (John 10:27-28).

12

Finding Christ as Our Relationship with Everything

"When once the soul has been brought to feel the reality of its condition before God — the depth of its ruin, guilt, and misery — its utter and hopeless bankruptcy, there can be no rest until the Holy Spirit reveals a full and an all-sufficient Christ to the heart. . . . There may be sorrow, pressure, conflict, exercise of soul, heaviness through manifold temptations, ups and downs, all sorts of trials and difficulties; but we feel persuaded that when a soul is really brought by God's Spirit to see the end of self and to rest in a full Christ, it finds a peace which can never be interrupted."

– C. H. Mackintosh

When we spend time with the Lord morning by morning, we find Christ as our relationship with everything. Once we are in Christ and Christ becomes our life, we have a new center, a new point of reference from which we relate to everything. In 2 Corinthians 5:17 Paul says, "If anyone is in Christ, he is a new creation; old things have passed away; behold, all things have become new." The old things that have passed away are the old relationships we had, with *self* as our center. Now the new things that have come are the new relationships we have, with *Christ* as our center. What is new in the new creation? A new relationship with everything, because Christ is our new center and point of reference.

When Christ is our life and center, His relationship with all things becomes *ours*. Before Christ came into us, we related to everything in our lives from our self. Now we relate to everything from Him as our center. Apart from Christ we do not have a proper relationship with anything. This is why the Lord said in John 15:5, "I am the vine, you are the branches. He who abides in Me, and I in him, bears much fruit; *for without Me you can do nothing.*"

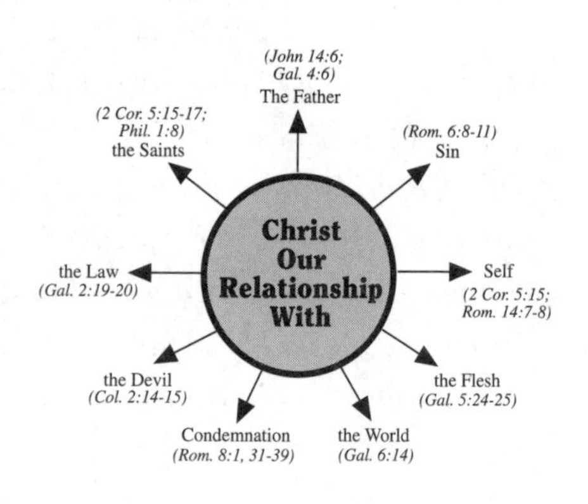

Christ is our relationship with *everything*—both positive and negative (as seen in the diagram). On the positive side, Christ is our relationship with the Father. He is also our relationship with all the saints, the members of His Body. On the negative side, Christ is our relationship with sin, the self, the flesh, the world, condemnation, the devil, and the law.

We must ask ourselves, How are we related to the Father? How are we related to the saints? How are we related to sin? How are we related to our flesh? How are we related to the world? Oftentimes we have tried to live the Christian life with ourselves as the source. But we must see that apart from Christ we have no life in ourselves (John 6:53). Our life is wholly wrapped up with Him. Our true life has been hidden with Christ in God. Christ is our life (Col. 3:3-4). This means that His history is our history: We died to sin *in Him,* we died to the flesh *in Him,* we died to the world *in Him,* we defeated the devil *in Him,* and we died to the law *in Him.* And now we live to the Father *in Him* and we relate to one another *in Him.* Our relationship with all these realms is Christ.

Let us consider what this means in our experience. How do we relate to the sins we've committed? We relate to our sins with the blood of Jesus (Heb. 10:17-19). How do we relate to our sin nature? We relate by what happened on the cross: Christ died to sin, and in Him we reckon ourselves to be dead to sin. We are alive to God *in Him* (Rom. 6:8-11). When we are oriented to these facts, our partaking of Christ, our participating in Him, becomes rich and full. He supplies to us the victory. The victory over sin and death is just Himself. We do not strive to win the victory. We receive and participate in His victory!

We are all on the same level, so we can all echo the familiar song, "Just as I am, without one plea, but that Thy blood was shed for me . . . O Lamb of God, I come, I come." This is exactly how we should relate to the Lord — always coming to Him *as we are.* If you are thinking that you have to do something about yourself — that you have to repair yourself or reach a point of being stronger in yourself to be accepted by God — then you have it all wrong. There is nothing in ourselves that can stand before God (Rom. 7:18). In fact, if we would try to clean ourselves up on our own and come to Him with some merit in ourselves, His analysis would be that all our righteousnesses are nothing but filthy rags (Isa. 64:6). God only accepts one Person — His only begotten Son.

When Christ is revealed in me (Gal. 1:15-16), I have a new relationship with everything. I no longer come from the source of myself. I am no longer the savior of my life. Christ Himself is my Savior. I no longer interact with matters and things apart from Him, as though I am on my own. As a man in Christ, I am in the realm of the new creation, where "all things are out of God" (2 Cor. 5:17-18). Because I have Christ as the center and spring of my life, I now have a new relationship with all things.

Christ — our relationship with the Father

We do not have a separate relationship with the Father apart from the Son's own relationship with Him. God is not establishing a new relationship with us. He has established one relationship — with His Son. And now He gives that relationship to us as a gift. This is the meaning of the gift of eternal life in the New Testament. Eternal life is receiving the Son of God into us and participating in His relationship with the Father. First John 5:20 says, "And we know that the Son of God has come and has given us an understanding, that we may know Him who is true; and we are in Him who is true, in His Son Jesus Christ. This is the true God and eternal life."

John 14:6 tells us that it is *through* Christ that we come to the Father. Jesus said, "I am the way, the truth, and the life. No one comes (Gk: is coming) to the Father except through Me."

We are not coming to the Father on our own. Galatians 4:6 gives us a more precise definition of Who is coming to the Father by saying, "God has sent forth the Spirit of His Son into your hearts, crying out, Abba, Father." We are coming to the Father with the Son Himself in our hearts crying, "Abba, Father." Our crying "Abba, Father" *is* Christ in us crying "Abba." He says "Abba" in our "Abba" (cf. Rom. 8:15). In other words, we are actually participating in Christ's own relationship with the Father.

When we receive eternal life we receive the Father and Son's very own relationship. Now Christ Himself is my relationship with the Father. You and I do not have a different relationship with God besides the one Christ has with the Father. This is why after the Lord revealed the one unique relationship in the universe between Himself and the Father, He immediately said, "Come to Me, all you who labor and are heavy laden, and I will give you rest" (see Matt. 11:27-30). This means there is no longer any need to labor and struggle, trying to establish our own relationship with God (Rom. 10:3-4). We only need to come to Jesus and learn from Him. When we do, we are joined to Him and discover that *our* relationship with the Father is actually *His* relationship. We are merging with His relationship with the Father, and this brings rest to our souls.

Because of redemption, God can now give away His relationship with His Son. Galatians 4:4-6 says, [4] "But when the fullness of the time had come, God sent forth His Son, born of a woman, born under the law, [5] to redeem those who were under the law, that we might receive the sonship. [6] And because you are sons, God has sent forth the Spirit of His Son into your hearts, crying out, Abba, Father!" To receive the sonship is to receive the rights, privileges, and relationship of the Son of God. Our God took His relationship with His Son and put it right into our hearts! Now we do not have a separate fellowship with the Father. Indeed, we have been called into the one unique fellowship of His Son, Jesus Christ our Lord (1 Cor. 1:9). "Truly our fellowship is with the Father and with His Son Jesus Christ" (1 John 1:3).

This relationship and fellowship means that we are not standing upon our own righteousness, but upon Christ's alone (1 Cor. 1:30). Neither are we dependent upon our condition or status as the basis of our relationship with God. We are not trusting in anything related to ourselves (Phil. 3:7-9). We are nothing and have nothing. So when we wake up in the morning we do not need to inspect *our* relationship with God. Rather we can say, "Lord Jesus, how are You doing today? How is *Your* relationship with the Father?" Never again do we need to doubt our relationship with God since our relationship with God is Christ (Rom. 8:38-39).

The uniqueness of the Lord's relationship with the Father is emphasized in John 14:6 when He says, "No one comes to the Father except through Me." When He says, "no one," it means categorically *no one* (Rom. 3:10-12). No one is coming to the Father except through Him. When He says, "I am the way, the truth, and the life," He is saying, "I am your constant relationship with the Father." So how could we ever sink to the level of morbid self-introspection again? That kind of inward, subjective activity is useless! It is wasted time and energy. My relationship with the Father is Jesus Christ. He doesn't change. Every morning I can wake up and open myself to God with a released spirit, knowing that my joy, my love, and my relationship with the Father is absolutely wonderful. Oh, what a Christ we have!

Christ — our relationship with sin

The New Testament reveals that Christ's relationship with sin has become our relationship. Christ is our relationship with sin. God dealt with sin *in Christ*. Then He put us in Christ. So now our relationship with sin is found in Christ. Romans 6:8-11 clearly shows us *how* Christ is our relationship with sin: [8] "Now if we died with Christ, we believe that we shall also live with Him, [9] knowing that Christ, having been raised from the dead, dies no more. Death no longer has dominion over Him. [10] For the death that He died, He died to sin once for all; but the life that He lives, He lives to God. [11] Likewise you also, reckon yourselves to be dead indeed to sin, but alive to God in Christ Jesus our Lord." Verse 11 says that we are "alive to God in Christ Jesus." This is a most astounding fact. I can declare with boldness by the Word of God that I am alive and living to God in Christ Jesus. This truth renews my mind regarding *how* I am alive to God! This is truth that sets us free!

On the positive side, we are alive to God in Christ Jesus; on the negative side, we are dead to sin. Since Christ died to sin once for all, His death to sin has now become my relationship to sin. There is no way to have a victorious relationship toward sin apart from Christ's relationship with it. Sin is a powerful force dwelling in our flesh (Rom. 7:14-24). To attempt in ourselves to overcome this indwelling sin is to end up in the same condition the apostle Paul experienced at the end of Romans 7 — defeated and wretched.

In Christ's crucifixion He died to sin once for all. Now in the realm of resurrection He lives to God. In the same way, we died to sin in His death and now in Him we also live to God in resurrection (Rom. 6:6-11). Our history, our life, and our existence are all bound up with Him. Thus, our relationship to sin is the same as His relationship to sin; that is, it is in the realm of resurrection life. He is living to God and we also are living to God in Him.

To be dead to sin implies that we are living in another realm. Just as a dead person is dead to the physical realm but alive to the after-life (Luke 16:19-31), so also we are dead to the realm of sin because we are alive in the realm of the Spirit and life. According to Romans 8:2, "The law of the Spirit of life in Christ Jesus has made me free from the law of sin and death." One realm frees us from another realm. Thus, being dead to sin has nothing to do with our impotent efforts and struggles to overcome sin. Rather, it is a question of what realm we are in.

When we see Christ as all in all; He then becomes not only our relationship with all things, but He also becomes the new realm in which we live. Indeed, the way we experience death to sin is not by trying in ourselves to be dead to it. It is by staying in the realm of resurrection. The realm of resurrection is the realm of the Spirit and life (1 Cor. 15:45). In this realm we are automatically freed from sin. The power of sin is broken in our lives by what one servant of the Lord has called "the expulsive power of a new affection." This new affection is in the realm of the Spirit. It is the love of God poured out in my heart by the Holy Spirit that enables me to put to death the practices of my body (Rom. 5:5; 8:13).

Dealing with sin is not achieved by struggling to overcome it. Rather, we deal with sin by drawing from the life-power of Christ in the realm of resurrection. Instead of interacting with sin as though it was my responsibility to overcome it in myself, I interact with Christ, who is my relationship with sin. In this relationship, sin is a dead thing to me. Because I can exercise my spirit, where I am alive to God in Christ, I come under the expulsive power of a new affection for God and the things of God (Rom. 8:5-6). It is that affection that immobilizes the force of sin in my life. So in the realm of the spirit, indwelling sin forever remains a dead thing to me, because I died and my *new me* is now hidden with Christ in God.

In Romans 6:11 Paul says to reckon ourselves to be "dead indeed to sin, but alive to God in Christ Jesus." The Greek word for "reckon" is *logizomai.* It is a mathematical term and can simply mean 2 + 2 = 4. Such an equation is reliable and can be counted upon every time we use our calculator to do some addition. By using the word "reckon," Paul wanted to convey that we can rely upon Christ as our relationship with sin just as we rely upon the facts of mathematics. For example, when you wake up in the morning and it is stormy weather outside and the electrical power has failed, it does not change the fact that 2 + 2 = 4. Whether it is good weather or bad weather, two plus two will always equal four.

In the realm of the Spirit, to reckon means to trust and rely upon what exists in that realm. What exists there? Victory over sin in Christ Jesus! No wonder Paul broke forth in Romans 7:25 and declared, "Thanks be to God *through* Jesus Christ our Lord!" At that moment he saw Christ as his relationship to sin. Sin could no longer intimidate him. He was freed from the torment of sin because he saw his new relationship with sin in the Person of Christ. Instead of living in the mode of being miserable and wretched, he started operating in the mode of thanksgiving. When we experience Christ in this way — as our relationship to sin — the church will become increasingly a life-giving expression of Him.

Christ — our relationship with the flesh

In John 3:6 the Lord Jesus said, "That which is born of the flesh is flesh, and that which is born of the Spirit is spirit." By using the Greek perfect tense (signifying a present, permanent state) for the word "born," He conveyed two important facts: first, the realm of the flesh never changes; and second, the realm of the Spirit never changes. These two realms are separate from each other. They are mutually exclusive and even oppose each other (Gal. 5:17).

When we receive Jesus Christ into our life, we need to realize that our flesh does not change at that time. Neither will it change in the future. Rather, when we receive Him, it is our spirit that is born again. Our dead spirit is begotten of the divine Spirit and comes alive (Eph. 2:1; Rom. 8:10). Indeed, our newly-born, mingled spirit becomes the source from which we live as believers. It is into our regenerated spirit that Christ comes to dwell. From this place He Himself becomes our relationship with the flesh. Thus, our relationship with the flesh is Jesus Christ *as He* lives in our spirit and *as we* walk according to spirit (Rom. 8:3-4).

There are many aspects of the flesh — the lusts of the flesh (Gal. 5:16), the will of the flesh (John 1:13), the mind of the flesh (Rom. 8:6-7), and the works of the flesh (Gal. 5:19), to name a few. The flesh has feelings and reactions, as well as deeds; and many times we are subject to these things. Thus, we have a close relationship with the flesh.

Concerning his own flesh, Paul had to admit, "For I know that in me (that is, in my flesh) nothing good dwells" (Rom. 7:18). Also, in Colossians he warns the believers that if they relate to the evil flesh with a religious flesh they will encounter certain defeat (Col. 2:18-23). How then can we be related to our flesh, if the flesh cannot overcome the flesh? The answer to this question is found in Galatians 5:24-25: [24] "And those who are of Christ Jesus have crucified the flesh with its passions and desires. [25] If we live in the Spirit, let us also walk in the Spirit." The phrase, "those who are of Christ Jesus," tells us how we are to be related to the flesh. It is simply by our belonging to Christ Jesus that the flesh is crucified.

Are you one who is "of Christ Jesus"? To be of Christ Jesus means that you do not have a separate life from Him. You are wholly identified with Him. You do not have a separate relationship with the flesh. Because you are of Christ Jesus, you *own* His relationship with the flesh. His relationship with the flesh is not a long, drawn-out battle with it; rather it is a one-time crucifixion to it. The word "crucified" in Galatians 5:24 is in the aorist tense in Greek, indicating that a blow was dealt to the flesh in the past that was decisive, complete, and final. That blow was dealt to the flesh on the cross of Calvary two thousand years ago.

How we are related to the flesh is wrapped up in the answer to one question — Are we of Christ Jesus? That is all we need to answer. We don't need to examine whether or not we have any potential to overcome the flesh. Neither do we need a good record or a string of victories that we can boast in. Nor do we need to look at our condition to see whether or not we feel like a crucified person. We just need to answer one question — Are we of Christ Jesus? If so, we have crucified the flesh. Paul says it — if we are of Christ Jesus then we have crucified the flesh. This means that Christ is our relationship with the flesh.

In Galatians 5:24 our relationship with the flesh is an established fact in Christ Jesus. Then verse 25 shows us the application and experience of this fact: "If we live in the Spirit, let us also walk in the Spirit." To "live in the Spirit" in this verse is equivalent to being "of Christ Jesus" in the preceding verse. Thus Christ, in the realm of the Spirit, is our relationship with the flesh. But for this fact to become our experience over and over again in our daily life, we need to walk in the Spirit.

The Greek word for "walk" in Galatians 5:25 is a specific military word, rather than the more general word for "walk" used in other places in the New Testament. It has the sense of "keeping in step with the Spirit." This could be likened to a group of soldiers marching down the street, keeping in step with the cadence of the drummer. Their steps are very deliberate and specific. It is the same when we walk in the spirit. Christ is in us, in our mingled spirit. He has already dealt a blow to the flesh. Now we must keep in step with Him whenever our flesh rises up to be fulfilled. This means we take a deliberate and specific step in spirit at the moment our flesh manifests itself. When we keep in step with the Spirit, the Lord Himself is our relationship with the reacting flesh. We just say, "Amen, Lord, I love You!" Or call out His name, "Lord Jesus!" By interacting with Him in this way, we keep in step with the Spirit and execute the crucifixion over our flesh.

The main point in dealing with the flesh is to not interact with it. We do not dare to handle it on our own. There is only One who is qualified to handle it, and He was incarnated to do so. He became flesh (John 1:14) and lived a victorious life in the flesh (Rom. 8:3). And now in resurrection He has become a life-giving Spirit in our spirit to supply to us His triumphant relationship over the flesh. All we need to do is keep in step with the Spirit—pray a little bit, call "Jesus" a little bit, shout to God a little bit, sing a little bit. Just keep in step with the Spirit.

You may say to me, "I can't overcome my flesh. I have already tried over and over again and failed." I will respond by saying, "That's right! Of course you can't!" If you and I have a relationship with the flesh based upon ourselves, we are finished. We all must come back to Christ—to see Him as our relationship with the flesh and then just keep in step with the Spirit.

Christ — our relationship with the world

When we as believers allow Christ to be our relationship with the world, we will find ourselves living in the realm of the "new creation" (2 Cor. 5:17; Gal. 6:15). This new creation is the church, also described in Colossians 3:10-11 as "the new man" where "Christ is all and in all." To have a practical church life in this realm requires a decisive dealing with the world — with both the evil world and the religious world. These two worlds are always opposing God's perfect will, which is to have the church as a pure expression of Christ (Gal. 1:4; Rom. 12:2; 1 John 2:15-17).

The apostle Paul speaks concerning his relationship with the world in Galatians 6:14-15: [14] "But God forbid that I should glory except in the cross of our Lord Jesus Christ, by whom the world has been crucified to me, and I to the world. [15] For in Christ Jesus neither circumcision nor uncircumcision avails anything, but a new creation." Paul lived in the realm of the new creation and experienced the crucified Christ as his relationship with the world. The cross of Christ was the point of reference for Paul by which the world was crucified to him and he to it. According to Paul, in these two verses "the world" is something opposite from the "new creation."

When our relationship to the world is Christ, we are crucified to the world and it to us. That means we are released to live in the new creation — in a different realm with different goals and values. In this realm, the system of the world under Satan's dominion is nullified. Our priorities are not the same.

Rather than being usurped by this age with its worldly preoccupations, our time and energy are for God's will and purpose.

When Christ is our relationship with the world, it issues in the church as the new creation. The church is the *ekklesia* (Gk: ἐκκλησία), which means the "called-out ones." This is the nature of the church — being assembled as the called-out ones. When I am out of the world, I am in the church. The fact that we could meet as the church means that we are out of the world. We are out of the world because Christ is out of the world (John 17:15-16).

The cross is our once-and-for-all dealing with the world. We are not trying in ourselves to deal with the world. It has been dealt with in Christ through His cross. Now we glory and boast in the cross of our Lord Jesus Christ, because by it the world has been crucified to us and we have been crucified to it. The world is a dead thing to us and we are a dead thing to it. We no longer live according to the world's values. Rather, we value the new creation, where Christ is all and in all.

Christ — our relationship with condemnation

Christ has also become our relationship with condemnation. Have you ever considered what your relationship with condemnation is? Many times we live under a stream of condemning thoughts from the enemy. We relate to these thoughts by coping with them in some way or another. Sometimes we try swatting them like flies. Or we attempt to replace them with new resolutions and promises to God that we won't fail again. Or we just sink into depression and we live feeling condemned.

God's answer to this spiritual disease is found in Romans 8:1: "There is therefore now no condemnation to those who are in Christ Jesus." In other words, not being condemned has nothing to do with your past record or your present performance. Nor is it dependent upon your ability to cope with your thoughts. It is strictly a matter of *where* you are. Where are you? Are you *in yourself* or are you *in Christ Jesus?* If you are in Christ Jesus, then you can shout "Hallelujah!" You can tell condemnation that you are now related to it in Christ. Because you are included and hidden in Him, all the arrows of condemnation have to come to Him. Of course, that is unthinkable! Christ cannot be condemned. So you cannot be condemned! Thus, you need not shrink back in coming to God. You can draw near to God through Him (Heb. 7:25).

Because Paul is so clear about being a person in Christ who cannot be condemned, he begins to boldly challenge everyone in the universe. It is as if he was saying, "Are you (whoever you may be) going to condemn me? Are you going to bring a charge against me? Come and listen to me!" In Romans 8:31-34 he declares, [31] "What then shall we say to these things? If God is for us, who can be against us? [32] He who did not spare His own Son, but delivered Him up for us all, how shall He not with Him also freely give us all things? [33] Who shall bring a charge against God's elect? It is God who justifies. [34] Who is he who condemns? It is Christ who died, and furthermore is also risen, who is even at the right hand of God, who also makes intercession for us."

Paul totally ignores the possibility of being chargeable or of the condemnation being legitimate. He does not give any ground for anyone to say anything against him. He does not answer the charges with himself, his record, or even his victorious Christian life. He only answers with Christ Jesus. It is Christ who died! It is Christ who is risen! It is Christ who is at the right hand of God making intercession for us! It is Christ who is our relationship with condemnation!

Our problem is that we have been in a relationship with condemnation for such a long time that we live with our conscience deflated and our spirit down. We can't enjoy God because we are flooded with condemning thoughts. At those points we have to boldly declare, "Condemnation, I don't have a relationship with you anymore. My relationship with you is now my Christ." We all need to learn this lesson from an older brother in the Lord. He is about 90 years old and ready to meet the Lord at any time. I heard him give the following testimony: "You know what I do when the devil comes and starts to condemn me? I say, JESUS! HE'S HERE AGAIN!" Oh, brothers and sisters, that is what we need to declare when those condemning thoughts come streaming in — "JESUS! HE'S HERE AGAIN! THE THOUGHTS ARE HERE AGAIN!" We don't handle condemnation with ourselves. We handle it with Christ, because He is now our relationship with it. Indeed, Christ is our relationship with everything!

Christ — our relationship with the devil

One of the most crucial areas in which we need to know Christ is our relationship with the devil. In Jude 9 we read, "Yet Michael the archangel, in contending with the devil, when he disputed about the body of Moses, dared not bring against him a reviling accusation, but said, 'The Lord rebuke you!' " Michael's relationship with the devil in this verse is brief and to the point — "The *Lord* rebuke you!" That says it all. The Lord Himself is our relationship with the devil.

At every stage of the Lord's history, He defeated the devil. *In His human life,* in the wilderness and in His ministry, He defeated him (Matt. 4:1-11; Luke 11:20-23). *In His death on the cross,* Christ decisively destroyed the devil and triumphed over him (John 12:31-33; Heb. 2:14; Col. 2:14-15). *In His resurrection,* Christ broke the devil's power (1 Pet. 3:18-22; Rev. 1:18). *In His ascension and enthronement,* He subdued the devil (Eph. 1:19-22). *In His building of the church,* He crushed Satan under our feet so that he cannot prevail (Rom. 16:20; Matt. 16:18-19). *In His indwelling* in the believer, Christ is greater than the devil (1 John 4:4). *In His battle to bring in the kingdom,* all believers overcome the devil because of the blood of the Lamb (Rev. 12:9-11). *In His millennial kingdom,* the devil is bound in the abyss for a thousand years (Rev. 20:1-3). *In His eternal victory,* the devil is cast into the lake of fire (Rev. 20:10). Hallelujah!

At any point in our daily life we can resist the devil by simply resting in the Object of our faith — our victorious

Christ (1 Pet. 5:8-9). By submitting to God with Christ our life, the devil has to flee (James 4:7). By being totally focused on Christ and remaining pure and simple toward Him, we keep ourselves preserved from the deceiving serpent so that he cannot touch us (2 Cor. 11:2-3; 1 John 5:18). What a victory! Christ is our relationship with the devil.

Christ — our relationship with the law

God desires that the church be the enlargement of Christ (Eph. 1:22-23). For this to happen God made Christ our wisdom and our relationship to everything (1 Cor. 1:30). Thus, the more we experience Christ as our relationship in all things, the more the church is Christ being fully expressed through His members. This includes the believers' relationship with the law. Christ is also our relationship with the law.

In Galatians 2:19-21 the apostle Paul shows how our relationship with the law is just Christ: [19] "For I through the law died to the law that I might live to God. [20] I have been crucified with Christ; it is no longer I who live, but Christ lives in me; and the life which I now live in the flesh I live by the faith of the Son of God, who loved me and gave Himself for me. [21] I do not set aside the grace of God; for if righteousness comes through the law, then Christ died in vain." In verse 19 we see how God dealt with us in our relationship to the law — we died to the law in the death of Christ on the cross. When Christ died on the cross we also died (2 Cor. 5:14). Indeed, Paul makes it clear in Romans 7:3-4 that when the body of

Christ was hanging on the cross, we not only died with Him but we died *to the law* with Him. The law demanded that the sinner die for his sin (Ezek. 18:4). Thus, in our co-crucifixion with Him, we legally and judicially died. We were all judged on the cross in His death. The law effectively put us to death in Him and dealt a final blow to our law-breaking flesh. This is the meaning of Paul's statement, "I through the law died to the law."

Now that we have died to the law in the death of Christ, we no longer have a relationship with it in ourselves. Our relationship to the law is now Jesus Christ Himself. He is not only the end of the law for righteousness to us (Rom. 10:4), but He is the fulfiller of the righteous requirement of the law in us as we walk according to spirit (Matt. 5:17-18; Rom. 8:3-4). We are no longer occupied with living to an impersonal law and demand that has no life in it. We are living to God in a Person who is life and who gives life! Christ being my relationship with the law means that it is no longer the law-keeping "I" who lives, but Christ who lives in me. This means I am forever delivered from slavery, bondage, legality, impotence, and fear. I am now living to God in the Person of Christ.

The way we live to God is not from ourselves or our efforts. We live to God in our relationship and our fellowship with His Son. In the Son we have received the "sonship" (Gal. 4:4-5). The "sonship" in the New Testament refers to an existence where we continually live before God as an object of His love (Eph. 1:4-6). We are being constantly supplied with grace because we are in the One who is continually being loved — the Beloved One! This is "sonship."

I live to God in the very relationship that Christ has with the Father (Eph. 2:18). Even though I am still in the flesh and can feel its tendencies and weaknesses, my relationship with God is never disturbed. This is because of a constant infusion of faith that comes from being so flooded with the personal love of my Christ for me. Paul says it well in Galatians 2:20: "the life which I now live in the flesh I live by the faith of the Son of God, who loved me and gave Himself for me." Thus, "the faith of the Son of God" was coming to Paul because of his love relationship with the Lord (Gal. 5:6). That is the way faith operates — it is simply by abiding in His love.

Despite the presence of the flesh and even the rumblings of the flesh, we are not under the law to interact with it or have any kind of relationship with it. The only thing we do now is keep ourselves in the love of God. By this we allow faith to keep infusing us to be completely occupied with Christ. It is in this way that the church is Christ — by saints being freed from the tyranny of the law, having only one relationship in their lives — Christ!

Christ — our relationship to ourselves
Concerning 2 Corinthians 5:14-15

One of the most wonderful things to discover is that once we have received Christ, He then becomes our relationship to ourselves. Paul makes this clear in 2 Corinthians 5:14-15: [14] "For the love of Christ constrains us, because we judge thus: that if One died for all, then all died; [15] and He died for all, that those who live should live no longer to themselves, but to

Him who died for them and rose again." In verse 14 when Paul says that "One died for all," according to our understanding, we probably would have continued the sentence by saying, "then all are forgiven." Of course, it is true in other passages of Scripture that when Christ died for all, He died to forgive all. However, in verse 14 Paul is stressing another aspect of Christ's death. The statement, "if One died for all, then all died," reveals a crucial fact about our relationship to ourselves. Furthermore, as we consider verse 15, Paul opens up what the issue should be of our having died in Christ's death — "that those who live should live no longer to themselves, but to Him." In other words, a relationship to ourselves with ourselves has ceased — Christ is now our true relationship to ourselves. We do not live to ourselves any longer. We live to Him.

The death of Christ is not only for our forgiveness; it is also for our termination. The terminating of the self is very positive, for it has one goal in view — the release of Christ living in us. When we no longer live to ourselves, we are no longer our point of reference in relation to our daily life and affairs. Our point of reference is no longer the self, but Christ. Thus, we begin learning how to live *to* Him. Who do we live to? Our orientation in our fallen nature is to live to ourselves — to our own reasoning mind, to our feelings, to our reactions, to our own analysis of ourselves. In the past "the self" has been our point of reference.

When the self is our point of reference, we really do not know ourselves as we should in God's light. In fact, according to the Scriptures, apart from Him we are prone to being deceived about ourselves. The self cannot accurately know the self. So no one really knows himself without God's light. Jeremiah 17:9 says, "The heart is deceitful above all things, and desperately wicked; who can know it?" Who can know their own heart properly? We may think we are fine, when we are totally off. Or we may think we are off, when we are fine. Brothers and sisters, we are unable to know our hearts. God says our hearts are desperately wicked, whether we agree with His diagnosis or not. It is God who asks the question, "Who can know the heart?"

In Jeremiah 17:10 the Lord answers His own question: "I, the LORD, search the heart, I test the mind, even to give every man according to his ways, and according to the fruit of his doings." It is the Lord who knows and searches our hearts. Even the Lord is identified by a compound title in Greek — "the Heart-Knower" (Acts 1:24; 15:8). Thus, to know ourselves we must first come to know God. We may think we know ourselves by introspection, or by analyzing our own heart. We may imagine that we know ourselves rightly, but apart from being in fellowship with the Heart-Knower, we are prone to deception.

Actually, James says it in a good way: "Draw near to God and He will draw near to you." And immediately after that he adds, "Cleanse your hands, you sinners; and purify your hearts, you double-minded" (4:8). Now, the religious way of understanding this verse is that *first* you cleanse your hands and try to purify your heart. You try to make it seem right, according to your thought. *Then* you draw near to God — as though you are the savior and the one who cleans yourself up, as though you are the one qualified to know the duplicity in your heart and to know when your heart is divided — as though you can do the work yourself!

You think that after you have done what you can, then you may draw near to God. But James does not say it that way. He says to come as you are and draw near to God. Come just the way you are, without one plea, but that His blood was shed for you. Blood has been shed. You can come the way you are, and God will draw near to you. And then you get in the light. "In Your light, we see light" (Psa. 36:9). In God's light your hands are dirty. "O God, look at the filth on me." And yet, when you are looking at your hands, you are not looking at them with yourself as the point of reference. You are looking at yourself from *His* light, and in His light the blood is cleansing. And you can weep and you can repent and you can shed tears; and all the time you are weeping and repenting and shedding tears, it is not at all ascetic or religious. You are actually participating in the grace of God.

Repentance is a gift (Acts 11:17-18). You do not work up repentance. Repentance is given to us as a gift (Ezek. 36:25-31). The fact that I could weep and repent and confess — that is a gift of God. Hallelujah! It is not of us. The whole thing is Him, from beginning to end. So we see that first, you draw near to God and He will draw near to you, and then you see your dirty hands and you see your heart — your motivation and how you manipulate people. You see the duplicity in your heart. You see how thoroughly corrupt you are. And all the time you see that, you say, "Lord, I still love You." And when you are saying that, He is just diffusing His life into your heart. He is going to change you. "I will take the heart of stone out of your flesh" (Ezek. 36:26). It is as though He is saying, "You can't do it. I will take it away. I will give you a new heart. I will give you a heart of flesh. And you will walk in My statutes. You will do it, because I am going to do it in you."

In one of our home meetings, there was a new sister among us. She was worn out as a believer and was ready to give up the Christian life. She had nowhere else to go. She sat in that meeting, just forlorn and disappointed. Raised in a Christian home, she had heard all the Christian teachings, but she did not know how to practically experience Christ in her life. I said to her, I am going to show you something. I opened to Ezekiel 36. She sat there, her face sad because she realized the condition of her heart, but had no way to handle it. I said, Look at what it says here, "I will give you a new heart and put a new spirit within you." Her tears were just starting to come down. I said, Look — "*I* will take away the stony heart." God is going to do it! She had never seen it before, that God would actually take away the stony heart. She began to weep for joy to see that it was God's work — He was going to do it.

"Draw near to God." You draw near, not after you adjust yourself, but before you even try. Because the blood has been shed, we can enter into God — the real Savior. He is the real Repairer. He is the real Healer. He is the One who cleans up our heart. He is the real Cleaner-upper. He is the real Restorer. He does it, and He does it while we are in contact with Him.

Being oriented to Christ in your experience means you are in contact with Him — no longer living to yourself but to Him. My point of reference is no longer me. My point of reference is Christ. For example, if I am broken down and I need some repair, then I need to go to the Repairman. Jesus is my Repairman. I do not know how to fix anything. I am just simple to come to Jesus. This is what I appreciate about my wife. She has her weaknesses, but amazingly, even in her frailty, weaknesses, and feelings of failure, she still has that boldness to just keep coming to God. Sometimes I wondered how she could be testifying in a meeting so boldly, when she was feeling so weak. But, you know, this is the right way — "Just as I am, without one plea . . . Fightings within and fears without, O Lamb of God, I come, I come." Amen. Just like that. And He does the work in us.

Concerning Romans 14:7-8

God wants us to keep coming forward and enjoy this grace that is ours. So our point of reference is not ourselves. It is Him. Romans 14:7-8 tells us, [7] "For none of us lives to himself, and no one dies to himself. [8] For if we live, we live to the Lord; and if we die, we die to the Lord. Therefore, whether we live or die, we are the Lord's." Then verse 9 continues, "For to this end Christ died and rose and lived again, that He might be Lord of both the dead and the living." It says, "that He might be Lord" — the Boss — "both of the dead and the living." So live to the Boss. Live to the Lord. He died and rose again, not merely to become a ticket in our pocket for us to go to heaven when we die. He died and rose again to be Lord. This means now we live to Christ. He is our point of reference. We no longer live to ourself. We never refer back to ourself. Our whole source has changed, from ourself to Him. He is bringing us back to what He intended with the tree of life in the garden of Eden — that He would be our source.

Our relationship with ourself is Christ. This kind of understanding will come progressively in our experience. As our mind is renewed by the Spirit and by the Word, a consciousness of life will begin to invade every area of our living. We will start linking this word with our experiences. For example, you may have a love of money in your heart, and you are not allowing the Lord to be the Lord with your finances. You are struggling over this matter. Then you begin to make the link with the Word — Christ is your point of reference. So now, you begin to touch Him, "Lord, Amen. You are my relationship with money. Jesus, thank You, You are the giving One in me. You are the life in me." You begin to drink and to eat Him in this way, and you begin to experience Him. You will discover that your greedy, closed hands will begin opening up, and you will start giving, even hilariously (2 Cor. 9:7), because Christ becomes your life.

This consciousness of Christ being our point of reference will continue to spread in our daily life. For example, you will find it in your speaking. You say something, but in your saying it, you feel like you put on a suit of clothes that doesn't fit, that doesn't feel right. As you are criticizing and gossiping, you are going to feel like, "O Lord, this language doesn't fit. Amen, Lord, You are my talk. You are my speaking. I used to speak so freely. But Lord, Amen." By contacting Him and experiencing Him in this way, you begin to feel the restraint in your words. Christ is becoming your talking (2 Cor. 13:3).

Little by little, the Holy Spirit will begin to make Christ real in your speaking. You may fail, but you experience Christ in your failure. You touch the living One because your point of reference has changed. You can no longer rearrange your thoughts, thinking, "I shouldn't talk that way anymore." Nor can you replace bad thoughts with good thoughts. That doesn't work! You have to interact with God. You have to touch the Spirit. And when you touch the Spirit, you draw from Him and He changes you. Then, you come to the meeting and you just make the meeting Christ — because you have handled Him. You have handled Christ as your portion in your speaking. Amen!

Christ — our relationship to one another

When Christ is our relationship to ourselves, and we know ourselves in God's light, the result of this knowing is that Christ becomes our relationship to one another. The apostle Paul follows this sequence in 2 Corinthians 5:14-17: [14] "For the love of Christ constrains us, because we judge thus: that if One died for all, then all died; [15] and He died for all, that those who live should live no longer to themselves, but to Him who died for them and rose again. [16] Therefore, from now on, we know no one according to the flesh. Even though we have known Christ according to the flesh, yet now we know Him thus no longer. [17] Therefore, if anyone is in Christ, he is a new creation; old things have passed away; behold, all things have become new." In verses 14 and 15 of this passage, Paul stresses that we no longer live to ourselves, based upon the fact that we all died in Christ. Then in verse 16 Paul goes directly into our relationship with one another. In other words, when we live to Christ rather than to ourselves, we know each other and are related to each other not according to the flesh, in the realm of the old creation, but in the spirit, in the realm of the new creation.

The deep significance of 2 Corinthians 5:16-17 is that Paul opens up a new kind of knowing of Christ in contrast to his old knowing of Christ. What is this new kind of knowing of Christ? The obvious answer is in verse 17, where Christ is presented in an enlarged way by Paul. He no longer considers Christ merely alone by Himself. He says, "*If anyone is in Christ,* he is a new creation . . ." Christ here is not just an individual man, but a corporate man where other persons are "in Him." Thus, the new knowing of Christ is knowing Him as the church (Eph. 5:29-30). It is the knowing of Him according to 1 Corinthians 12:12, where both the one body and the many members form one whole Christ! It is also the same knowing of Him found in Paul's prayer for the believers in Ephesians 1:17-23. Here, the full knowledge of God is to know Christ as the Head of His Body, the church, which is described as being "the fullness of the One who fills all in all."

It is the church as Christ that is the new kind of knowing of Christ in 2 Corinthians 5:16. The church described as "the new man" in Colossians 3:10-11 is also the new kind of knowing of Christ. The church as the new man of the new creation is the realm where Christ is all and in all. It is also the realm where old things have passed away and all things have become new! In this realm we know each other as members of Christ. We no longer regard or know each other according to the differences and distinctions of the old creation (Gal. 3:27-28).

According to the context of 2 Corinthians 5, to say "old things have passed away" and "all things have become new" means that old relationships have passed away and all things in our relationships with each other have become new. *Together* we all have been newly created in Christ as one new man, and have all been reconciled to God in one body by the cross (Eph. 2:15-16).

Christ as our relationship with each other is what the church is. In other words, the church is just Christ between us. If Christ is not our mutual fellowship, then the reality of the church is lost. So, brothers and sisters, to know the church is to know Christ as our relationship with each other. It is not a matter of knowing each other in a natural way according to race or background. Neither is it formally joining a church to become a member. No. We are joined to the Lord in one Body, and His relationship with all His members becomes our relationship with every member. So we freely receive one another the way Christ received us (Rom. 15:7). This is what the church is. Praise the Lord!

The depths and intimacy of Christ as our relationship with one another comes out in Paul's relationship with the Philippians. In Philippians 1:8 we read, "For God is my witness, how greatly I long for you all with the inward parts of Jesus Christ." Here Paul so identifies his feelings with the Lord's that he is not merely saying, "I am burdened for you" or "I am thinking of you." The Lord Himself with His inward parts became Paul's relationship with the Philippians. Paul was a man who embodied the Lord's own feelings and intimate care for the saints. This demonstrates to what extent Christ becomes our relationship with one another. My relationship with you and your relationship with me is Christ. How precious this is. The more there is an increase of Christ in us, the more there will be an increase of Christ in our relationships. Amen.

13

Giving the Lord the First Place

"Whatever we need and whatever we lack is in God, and in our Lord Jesus Christ, in whom the Father willed all the fullness of His bounty to abide (cf. Col. 1:19; John 1:16) so that we may all draw from it as from an overflowing spring. It remains for us to seek in Him, and in prayers to ask of Him, what we have learned to be in Him. Otherwise, to know God as the Master and Bestower of all good things, who invites us to request them of Him, and still not go to Him and not ask of Him — this would be of as little profit as for a man to neglect a treasure, buried and hidden in the earth, after it had been pointed out to him. Accordingly, the apostle, in order to show that true faith cannot be indifferent about calling upon God, has laid down this order: just as faith is born from the gospel, so through it our hearts are trained to call upon God's name (Rom. 10:14-17). And this is precisely what he had said a little before: the Spirit of adoption, who seals the witness of the gospel in our hearts (Rom. 8:16), raises up our spirits to dare show forth to God their desires, to stir up unspeakable groanings (Rom. 8:26), and confidently cry, 'Abba! Father!'" (Rom. 8:15).

– John Calvin

All the fullness concentrated in Christ

All the fullness was pleased to be concentrated in Christ. This is the most awesome revelation of Christ — that in Him all the fullness was pleased to dwell (Col. 1:19). It is the same as saying there is nothing outside of Christ. Don't go outside of Christ. Don't even take a little trip someplace else, someplace apart from Him, be it to your self-life, be it to anything of the world, anything that fascinates you. Don't go outside of Him. Don't look at yourself outside of Him. Don't contemplate yourself outside of Him. There is nothing outside of Him.

The revelation of Christ as the concentration of all the fullness is the communication of a burden that Christ would so totally be all to us that we just finding ourselves falling into His arms over and over again. Just as John 1:18 says: We are "into the bosom of the Father," into that love-life over and over again, whatever we may be passing through. It is as if the Father is saying, "My Son is the concentration and focus of all the fullness in this universe." This tells us that before any kind of history took place, the Father designated that the fullness of everything would dwell in His Son. That is how much Christ is "front and center." And the reconciliation of this universe is happening wherever Christ is supreme, exalted, has first place, is the theme, is the atmosphere, is the conversation, is the love, is the glory, is the majesty. What God is doing in this universe is exalting and magnifying His Son, Christ. This is His pleasure. So we need to be taken totally out of ourself by being enthralled and occupied exclusively with the Son of God.

"All the fullness" as a personified phrase

One of the most revealing verses in the entire Bible is Colossians 1:19. This is because it unveils from God's perspective the one unique pleasure of the universe. It says, "Because in Him all the fullness was pleased to dwell." *All the fullness* is a comprehensive phrase that includes all the major things in the universe, depicted in the diagram. These things include the Godhead, eternity past, creation,

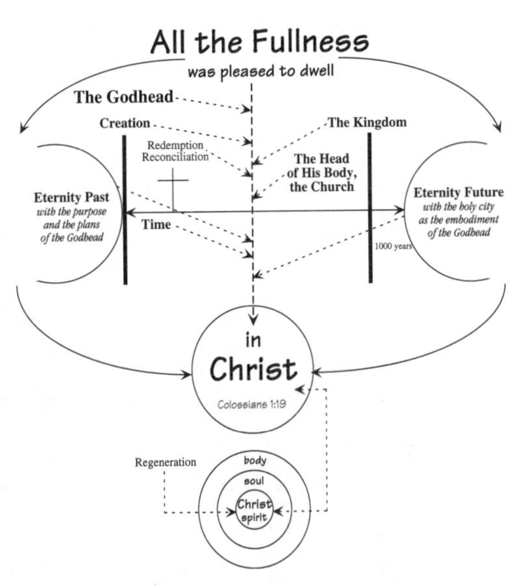

time, redemption, the church, the kingdom, and eternity future. All this fullness was pleased to dwell in one place — Christ. Thus, Christ is the focal point and concentration of the pleasure of all the fullness in this universe. If we see with the eyes of our heart the truth and reality of this verse, it will impact our lives in the most profound way, as nothing else could.

The first thing we must do is seek to understand what Colossians 1:19 actually says. The literal Greek should be translated, [ὅτι *(hoti)* = because] in Him all the fullness was pleased to dwell." In this unique utterance *all the fullness* is personified. R. C. H. Lenski, in his commentary on Colossians, observes the grammatical significance of this phrase: "It is not necessary that 'all the fullness' have a specifying genitive [e.g., 'of God'] because this fullness itself is personified by what is predicated of it in the verb *[was pleased]* plus its infinitives *[to dwell* and *to reconcile]* and participle *[having made peace]*." Thus, all the fullness is characterized as having a feeling — a pleasure. This personification of all the fullness reveals not only the Personhood of the Godhead but the entire economy of the Godhead, including all Their purposes, plans, counsels, and acts from eternity past to eternity future. This point is confirmed by M. R. Vincent in his *Word Studies in the New Testament:* "Thus the phrase *in Him should all the fullness dwell* gathers into a grand climax the previous statements [from Col.1:15-18] — *image of God, first-born of all creation, Creator, the eternally preexistent, the Head of the Church, the victor over death, first in all things*. On this summit we pause, looking, like John, from Christ in His fullness of deity to the exhibition of that divine fullness in redemption consummated in heaven (vv. 20-22)."

To personify all the fullness by making it the subject of the verb, *was pleased,* is in contrast to most of the English translations of the New Testament, and it is also in contrast to the way many Bible commentators have sought to interpret it. For example, both the *King James Version* and the *New King James Version* insert "the Father" as the subject of the verb *was pleased.* The *New King James Version* says, "For it pleased the Father that in Him all the fullness should dwell."

But it is important to notice that *the Father* is italicized, indicating that these words are not in the original text, but are inserted by the translator in an attempt to make the thought more understandable. Of course, according to the truths revealed in the Bible concerning the Godhead, there is no problem with that translation. Theologically, it is accurate to say, "It pleased the Father that in Him all the fullness should dwell." But this is not what the text in Colossians 1:19 says. Inserting "the Father" is an interpretation and not a translation of the Greek text. *The New Translation* by J. N. Darby says, "For in Him all the fullness [of the Godhead] was pleased to dwell." Darby translates the verse literally, but inserts his interpretation in brackets.

One of the predicaments in translating the Bible is that at certain points the systematic theology of the translator may limit him because it can bring in a preconceived notion or thought. For example, in coming to a verse that is difficult to understand, he may interpret the verse so as to fit into a systematized body of truth. In some cases this is necessary and legitimate because it maintains the harmony of the whole Bible. In other cases, as here in Colossians 1:19, the translator may miss an awesome revelation of the greatness of Christ. So it is best not to impose our own thought on the Bible. Our lack of understanding may simply be due to the fact that we fail to possess the same revelation the apostle Paul had. This, I believe, is the case in handling Colossians 1:19. Paul was expressing the immensity and enormity of the centrality of Christ in the universe, and the only way he could express it was by saying, "In Him all the fullness was pleased to dwell."

Verse 19 should be literally translated according to the grammar: "Because in Him all the fullness was pleased to dwell." The words "was pleased" are the verb. And the subject of this verb is "all the fullness." "All the fullness was pleased to dwell." The *Rotherham Emphasized Bible* gives us a faithful translation by saying, "Because in Him was all the fullness well pleased to dwell." *Young's Literal Translation of the Bible* also renders this verse accurately: "Because in Him it did please all the fullness to tabernacle." This is hard for us to grasp because it is not according to our natural concept. Nevertheless, it is something that God wants to convey to us to show us how vast Christ is.

There are a number of other distinguished scholars and Bible teachers who confirm the thought of all the fullness being a personification. For example, in *The Cambridge Greek Testament,* A. Lukyn Williams comments on the phrase *all the fullness:* "If all the fullness (πᾶν τὸ πλήρωμα) be the subject, more is attributed to what is impersonal than we should expect." In other words, at first glance we would mistakenly view all the fullness as being impersonal, and therefore would not attribute something personal — "was pleased" — to it. Thus, perceiving the personification of the phrase *all the fullness* broadens the scope of its application and of our expectation. Williams goes on to say, "Colossians 2:9 is parallel only in form, for there it is only said that the fullness dwells in Christ, not that the fullness exercises pleasure and determination, and even reconciles (Col. 1:20)." Here he acknowledges the personification of all the fullness by connecting it with the two infinitives, to dwell and to reconcile: "For in Him all the fullness was pleased *to dwell* and through Him *to reconcile* all things to Himself." Both infinitives go with *all the fullness*. All the fullness dwells, and all the fullness reconciles. So *all the fullness* is an all-inclusive utterance of the Holy Spirit that brings us back into the context of Colossians chapter 1 to see all that is included in this fullness. The context will help us understand the significance of all the fullness.

The unique reason Christ has first place in all things

Colossians 1:18 says, "That He Himself might have the first place in all things." A more literal translation would be, "So that in all things He Himself becomes the first place." He *becomes* the first place in all things. Then we see that verses 18 and 19 are connected by the word "because." This little "because" assigns *the reason why* Christ has become first place in all things. It is "*Because* in Him all the fullness was pleased to dwell." Again, R. C. H. Lenski helps us understand this connection. Speaking of the conjunction "because," he says, "ὅτι *[hoti]* states the evidential reason by which we know that the God-man is what verse 18 states he is; it corresponds to ὅτι *[hoti]* occurring in verse 16, which is to be understood in the same sense." Thus, the thoughts in verses 18 and 19 must be taken together. All the fullness being pleased to dwell in Christ *is* the unique reason He has the first place in all things. This is what practically motivates us for Christ to become first place in all things in our experience. The pure revelation of such fullness dwelling in Christ produces in us *the reason* for Him to have first place in all things.

Do we know why Christ has first place in our life? Oh, brothers and sisters, it is *because* in Him all the fullness was pleased to dwell. It is not even because *I* think *I* need to give Him first place. It is not because I have been so bad and wayward. It is not because I am so rebellious. It is not because I need to get it together and give my all. This is like kicking a donkey — "Come on now. Get going! You've been in one place too long. Now get on with it!" That is not the reason. No, He has first place because of one unique reason — "Because in Him all the fullness was pleased to dwell." This is revelation. This is light concerning what motivates us to give all to the Lord and let Him be the first place in all things. This is saying, "Lord, You have the first place because You *are* the first place. *Before* I was born, *before* I had a history, *before* there was my failing condition, *before* all the considerations of my subjective self, it was the delight and pleasure of all the fullness that all the positive things in the universe be concentrated and permanently dwell in You." This is the unique reason why Christ has the first place in all things. This is the unique reason why I give Him first place in my life.

The deep significance of "all" in God's thought

Let me illustrate how Christ is all. Consider Christ as a large bowl filled with many items. Look into this bowl. Behold *all the fullness* in this bowl. The Godhead is in this bowl. Eternity past is in this bowl. All creation is in this bowl. Time is in this bowl. Redemption is in this bowl. The church is in this bowl.

The kingdom is in this bowl. Eternity future is in this bowl. These are the items that compose all the fullness. All these items together make up all the fullness. They all have only one unique pleasure, that is, to dwell in this bowl — God's Christ!

This is the deep significance of *all* in God's thought. In our thought *all* may be limited to things like all my money, all my time, all my future, all my material possessions. That may be the extent of what all means to us. But in God's thought, all means all the fullness dwelling in Christ. The revelation of all from God's view — that *all* is concentrated in Christ — will radically change our life. We will be a person who sees that the meaning of our very existence is in this One in whom all the fullness is concentrated and embodied. Then we know what we were made for and what the universe was made for. This is how high and how immense our Christ is. He is more majestic than we could ever imagine. He is beyond what we could ever conceive.

How big is our God?

Let me give a personal testimony of finding a bigger God in my experience. It happened over thirty-five years ago when I was dealing with the Lord about giving my all to Him. I remember so clearly when the Lord spoke to me to burn my sermons. To me that was a step of surrendering all. There was a struggle. It was like I was giving up my life — indeed, it was *my* life that was wrapped up in those sermons. My God was too small. I confined Him to the little blue cards I had typed for Sunday mornings. They were carefully prepared and alliteratively outlined, and if I lost those cards, I just did not know what I would say. I was so riveted to my sermon notes that God was restricted to them. I had spent thirty hours preparing each of those cards. Then the Lord said, "Burn them."

My God at that time was limited to a little blue sermon card. I only experienced a blue-card God. He was narrowed to that one little thing. When He spoke to me to burn my sermons, He also said, "Do not use any more notes when you speak." I was so riveted to those notes that the dealing over them was an intense struggle for a period of time. It was like *my* life was going out the door into the incinerator. I definitely felt like I was losing something. Of course, that is the way the soul life feels. It always feels like it is losing something. So read your symptoms and find out where you are. When you are feeling like you are going to lose something, that is a symptom. It is just a symptom of the soul. The self cannot help but feel that way. In fact, it is programmed that way. And we feel that consciousness in us. That is why there is a tug-of-war. You can feel the tug of that contrary self-life.

But what happened to me was that I exchanged my little measly all and I got *His all*. And from that point, I remember getting up to speak without one note. I had been enjoying God all week long in the Word, and I was sitting there on the platform, waiting to get up to share. I was thinking, "God, what am I going to say? I have so many things to say." The light in the Word was everywhere. The fresh flow of the Spirit was in my heart. I had found a larger God. I found a bigger God than I had known, a God who could supply and energize. This is what can happen to us when there are those little struggle points in our life and we just let our all go and take His all. The struggle seems so real to you, but don't be bothered. God is stretching your capacity so that He would be more of the fullness to you. This is our God.

We have to see how rich and full God wants to make Christ in our experience. If we see what a big Christ we have — that all the fullness was pleased to dwell in Him — we will easily and readily give Him first place in all things. We will enjoy the riches of Christ in a way that we have never known, in a way that transcends our piddly efforts, in a way above and beyond what we have eked out in our Christian life up to now.

The excellency of the knowledge of Christ

The apostle Paul gave Christ first place in all things. Otherwise, how could he have such a testimony, saying, "I count all things as *dung*"? Where did he get that word? It is translated in various ways in English — dung, refuse, rubbish, worthless trash. "Dung" is a word the Holy Spirit used from the experience of a man who was under the revelation of the excellency of the knowledge of Christ Jesus his Lord. I have often felt, "Dear Lord, I would like to get into a crevice of Paul's heart. I want to know the kind of Christ he knew." In Philippians 3:8-9 he declares, [8] "But moreover I also count all things to be loss on account of the excellency of the knowledge of Christ Jesus my Lord, on account of whom I have suffered the loss of all things and count them as refuse that I may gain Christ [9] and be found in Him, not having my own righteousness which is out of the law, but that which is through the faith of Christ, the righteousness which is out of God and based on faith." Paul did not want to have even a shred of his own righteousness. He was saying, "I do not want anything in myself that could boast or merit something or establish something before God and feel satisfied that I did something. I do not want one bit of my righteousness. I want the righteousness which is of God by faith, *that I may know Him*" (Phil. 3:10). Thus, standing in Christ as all my righteousness is the key to knowing Him in an ever-deepening way. I want to know Him and all that He is as He lives in me and operates in me. I do not want to be satisfied with my own man-made righteousness proceeding from myself. I want to know Him.

Do we see this? This is the testimony of a man who sees Christ in such a way that all else fades away into oblivion. This is the revelation of Christ given to us in Colossians chapter 1. It is the kind of vision where we see that in Him all the fullness was pleased to dwell. Such a seeing of Christ has the power to become the unique reason for Christ to be first place in all things in our lives. Oh, we need to see such an immense Christ!

The transmittable and executable Christ

Now this Christ is transmittable and executable. This is because He was processed through His incarnation, human living, death, resurrection, and ascension. Christ was identified with every kind of temptation that we touch in our daily life. He defeated every foe and won every battle with the world, the flesh, and the devil. Not only that, He conquered death itself and became in resurrection a life-giving Spirit, so that all the residing fullness in Him is transmittable to us. Now Christ can be instantly executed from within our spirit.

In regeneration our spirit was joined to the Lord, making possible the direct transmission of His life into us (1 Cor. 6:17; 15:45). Oh, what a vision — that such a Person has now become One who is on our level, and not only on our level, but on our level inside of us. Now in our spirit, when we pray and sing and just join ourselves with this One, then all the fullness that has been pleased to dwell in Him, including God's essence and nature, is transmitted into our being so that He not only transforms our soul but He gives life to our mortal bodies.

This is our Christ today. All the fullness concentrated in Him is transmittable to us and executable in us and for us (Col. 1:19; 2:9-10). This means Christ is all-sufficient to us. The more we see how all the fullness was pleased to dwell in Him, the more He will be all-sufficient to us. What happens with such an awesome revelation of Christ is that we discover His all-sufficiency. That is the net effect over our being — His life is sufficient for everything. This all-sufficiency of Christ is over us that we might experience all that He is in His immense and expansive fullness.

The discerning ability of seeing the all-sufficiency of Christ

Because Paul saw such an all-sufficient Christ, he could deal with the distractions that entered in among the Colossian believers: "Beware that no one carries you off as spoil through his philosophy and empty deceit, according to the tradition of men, according to the elements of the world, and not according to Christ" (2:8). Look at Paul's discernment concerning things that distract from Christ. Once you see Christ the way God sees Christ, you will have an automatic discernment concerning the things that differ from Christ and are substitutes for Him (cf. Phil. 1:9-10). It is not a matter of judging or condemning anything or anyone. It is a matter of discerning.

When you are under the revelation of the all-sufficiency of Christ and you see that in Him all the fullness was pleased to dwell, you can evaluate everything. The revelation has discerning ability. It discerns the emphasis today in the whole professing Christian world. It discerns the Christian magazines. It discerns the stories and reports circulating in the Christian world. It discerns the focus of all the Christian activities and seminars. It discerns the Christian bookstores. It discerns the "how-to" books, the psychology books, even the books on handling your money and having a better marriage. I do not mean that God cannot be in all these things, but I am saying that so many believers today are focused on these kinds of things, and the all-sufficiency of Christ is diminished. There is not a taste and an aroma of Christ. Instead, it is a philosophy. It is a *way* of doing things. It is methods, procedures, and principles to live by. It is adjusting your life. It is solving your problems. We cannot say that all these things are bad. They may be good. But good is not necessarily God. From the very beginning of the Bible, there was the tree of the knowledge of *good* and evil, signifying an independent self-life with Satan as its source.

In Colossians 2:8 Paul is burdened to warn believers of the distractions so that no one would carry them off through these substitutes, which are not according to Christ. What are we according to? We must be according to Christ. In verse 9 Paul assigns the reason *why* we should be according to Christ: "For in Him dwells all the fullness of the Godhead bodily." The conjunction "for" can also be translated "because." It is the same conjunction, ὅτι *[hoti]*, used in Colossians 1:19, which tells us *why* Christ has the first place in all things.

In Colossians 2:8-9 Paul gives us a clear comparison. He compares the Christ who embodies the fullness of the Godhead with the superficial realm of philosophy, empty deceit, the tradition of men, and the elements of the world. This comparison shows us that the real fullness of our life is to be found in being completely occupied with the Person of Jesus Christ. Fullness is not found anywhere else but in Christ. All the fullness in Colossians 1:19 includes the fullness of the Godhead dwelling in Him bodily in Colossians 2:9. And not only is the Godhead, in Their *existence,* part of all the fullness, but the entire *economy* of the Godhead is also part of all the fullness.

We are made full in Him

Paul continues in verse 10: "And you have been made full in Him, who is the Head of all rule and authority." The word "fullness" in verse 9 and the words "made full" in verse 10 come from the same Greek word. Thus, Paul first reveals Christ as the embodiment of all the fullness, and then he says, "And you have been made full in Him." The verb "have been made full" is in the perfect tense — the tense that describes a permanent state of being. So it can mean that even with all the philosophy, tradition of men, and other distracting things, even with your hearts broken and suffering due to these kinds of things (2:2), you are still presently in a state of fullness in Him.

Christ is your real point of reference; you are made full in Him. All the fullness dwells in Him, and you are in Him. So we do not *arrive* at fullness. We do not stretch forth and seek to somehow attain fullness. We start out in fullness because we are joined to fullness — we are joined to Christ — and fullness is our life (Col. 3:4). Fullness is our permanent state. Fullness is our real situation. Are you not in Christ? Is your spirit not intertwined and joined with the One in whom dwells all the fullness of the Godhead bodily? Are you not right now joined to Christ in your spirit? Now, what will you relate to when you wake up in the morning? Will you relate to the self, with all the thoughts and feelings of the soul life? Or will you relate to your real life? When you relate to Christ, your real life, you relate to your state of fullness. Thus, our constant point of reference is always Christ. Our beginning is Christ. We do not travel to reach Christ. He is our starting point. I do not care where I am or how I am — on the floor, under the floor, or up against a wall. My starting point is always Christ, where all the fullness dwells.

Practically in our experience we must see that all the fullness includes all the fullness of the Godhead and that we are made full in that fullness. That fullness is described in John 17:10, where Jesus says, "And all things that are Mine are

Thine, and Thine are Mine; and I have been glorified in them." This means the fullness in the Godhead is being transmitted into us. We are made full with the riches of Their nature and essence. Jesus is glorified *in* us. That is why it is so utterly important to be done with a life of introspection. In this fullness we are through with morbid introspection over ourselves — analyzing the self, our failures, and our fears about the future. We must be done with that kind of life and ever keep our spirit in its proper order — fixed on Christ. This is what Paul is saying in Colossians 2:5: "I am with you in spirit, rejoicing to see your good order and the steadfastness of your faith in Christ." Our order is faith in the Person who is our fullness. This is the proper order of our being. Our order is our enjoyment of the fullness of Christ, where we receive grace upon grace (John 1:16). We receive His all. With Christ, God freely gives us all things (Rom. 8:32).

Giving our all for His all

Who would not give all for this? All includes everything. It includes every emotion, every reaction, every kind of environment that we cope with, the hopeless feelings that sweep over our soul, the depression that seizes us. Nothing is as bad and wrenching as depression. It grips you like a vice so that your feelings seemingly cannot rise. Depression is a horrible state to be in. But we can even surrender that state to the Lord. Who can get out of that state? We bring our state to Him by calling upon His name (cf. Lam. 3:52-57). In that call — "Jesus" — is the revelation of all the fullness that was pleased to dwell in Him. That fullness met death and conquered it. It broke through demonic regions and realms. It defeated every region of the enemy's domain. And whether I feel His victory or I don't feel it, I declare that Name. Whether I have an instantaneous change or I don't have any change, I speak that Name. We do not walk by sight. We walk by faith. Sight is what we see. Sight is what we can feel. It may be that to us God is our own subjective feeling. But God is not our feeling. God is God. So by faith we say, "Thank You, Jesus, You are the Victor. You broke through the regions of death and hell and Hades. You broke through it all. Now You are far above all to be my all."

It is an awesome thing to see that in Christ all the fullness was pleased to dwell. Included in that fullness is all that He has accomplished in God's economy. And now in Him we are in a state of fullness because we are drawing our resources out of His fullness. The Christian life is nothing but a life of grace — grace in exchange for grace. What a Christ!

Eternity past is included in all the fullness

In Colossians 1:17 Paul says, "And He is before all things." The word "before" takes us into eternity past. Christ is before all things in eternity past. To see that eternity past is part of all the fullness that was pleased to dwell in Christ, we need to look at 2 Timothy 1:9, which says, "[God] who has saved us and called us with a holy calling, not according to our works but according to His own purpose and grace, which was given to us in Christ Jesus before the times of the ages." Our salvation and calling today are according to God's purpose and grace, which go back to eternity past — "before the times of the ages" — where everything was bestowed upon us in Christ Jesus. So we can see that the totality of all God's plans and counsels over us in eternity past was pleased to dwell exclusively in Christ.

Oftentimes I have come to the Lord and said, "Lord, I did not start this." I have talked to Him in this way. I have said to Him, "I did not call me. It was not me that called me. You saved me and called me. This is Your doing, Lord. You have done it. I know that You got involved with a mess when You got involved with me, and I admit it and I confess it, but I did not start it." I can talk with the Lord in this way because all the fullness that was pleased to dwell in Christ includes every transaction, every counsel, in the Godhead that took place before the world was. And in those counsels the Son agreed to take you and me just as we are and do a full clean-up job on us.

All the fullness includes the counsels in eternity past between the Father and the Son in which the Father gave us to the Son (John 10:29). The Son took us. We have all been committed to the Son's keeping. So those eternal counsels in the Godhead concerning us make up part of all the fullness in the universe. All those eternal counsels were pleased to dwell in Christ. So you cannot separate God's plans, purposes, eternal choice, predestination, and foreknowledge from Christ. The Christ who is in me and the Christ who is in you has known us from eternity past by name. And He stretched out a plan over us that takes us into eternity future. Actually, He has already seen us there, because John saw the holy city (Rev.

21—22). And the Lord has also seen Peter there. This means He saw beyond Peter's denials, He saw beyond Peter's rejections, He saw beyond Peter's hypocrisy — He saw beyond it all — and He saw Peter there as one of the foundation stones in the holy city. This is because all the fullness of the eternal counsels over Peter's life dwells in a Christ who not only saves, but keeps and protects and shepherds all the way into eternity future. What security we have in Christ!

Often we are only looking at what is about an inch from our nose. But when you touch Christ, you touch the eternal counsels that were given to Him and that He is now working out over us. So when you are uptight and right in the middle of wondering what is going to happen next — "What is he going to say when he comes home?" or "How are we going to make ends meet?" — you need to bypass the anxiety by calling upon His name — "Jesus." And when you speak that name, you get all the fullness that dwells in that name. That means the counsels of eternity past are there. Don't just look at what is immediate to you. Touch something of the fullness in Christ, where you see your present situation as part of God's eternal purpose over you to conform you to the image of His Son. Because all the fullness is concentrated in Christ, when we touch Him we touch the counsels, plans, and purposes of eternity past. And this realm is available to us in the Spirit. This is why Paul follows up the section about touching the Spirit in Romans 8:15-16 with verse 18: "For I consider that the sufferings of this present time are not worthy to be compared with the glory which shall be revealed in us." The things of "this present time" are swallowed up by all the fullness of eternity past and eternity future dwelling in Him as our "present portion."

Creation is included in all the fullness

In Colossians 1:15-16 we clearly see how creation is part of all the fullness that dwells in Christ. Speaking of Christ as "the Son of His love," Paul says, [15] "Who is the image of the invisible God, the Firstborn of all creation, [16] because *in* Him all things were created, in the heavens and on the earth, the visible and the invisible, whether thrones or lordships or rulers or authorities; all things have been created *through* Him and *unto* Him." The three italicized prepositions, *in* Him, *through* Him, and *unto* Him, reveal how all the fullness in creation is concentrated in Christ. And John 1:1 and 3 also say, [1] "In the beginning was the Word, and the Word was with God, and the Word was God. . . . [3] All things came into being through Him, and apart from Him not one thing came into being which has come into being." Absolutely everything came into being through Christ. So all the fullness embodied in this Person includes creation itself.

In the creation of the universe God did not want to commence anything or touch anything apart from His Son. This is how significant Christ is to the Father. He did not handle one thing apart from His Son. And as we have ministered in years past, if the Father does not handle anything, if the Father does not touch anything, apart from the Son, who are we to handle our emotion, thought, or reaction? Who are we to intrude? Who are we to handle our life apart from Christ?

According to Colossians 2:19, to handle Christ is to hold the Head. The Colossian believers were being influenced and deceived, and they were on the verge of being carried off. Then Paul exposed the real problem — certain ones were not holding the Head. The word "hold" in Greek means to seize with a firm grip. This shows how much we need to firmly stay with Christ and let Him be everything — how much we need to process everything through Him. So Paul used the Colossians' situation to reveal *why* we need to hold the Head — because Christ is inherent and central in everything, and all the fullness expressed in creation was pleased to dwell in Him.

Time is included in all the fullness

All the fullness includes not only creation, but also time itself and the present state of the universe. In Colossians 1:17 Paul makes an awesome statement about time and our present existence: "And He is before all things, and in Him all things consist." The word "consist" can also be translated "cohere," and it implies a uniting bond, or cohesiveness. The existence of time and the universe is being sustained and held together in Christ. Christ is the cohesive factor of the universe. Not only so, He is also the cohesive factor between us as believers. Ephesians 2:14 says, "He Himself is our peace." And Ephesians 4:3 says, "Being diligent to keep the oneness of the Spirit in the uniting bond of peace." So the nature of the cohesiveness of Christ between us is peace. It is peace that unites us, and this peace is Christ Himself between us.

The fact that all the fullness was pleased to dwell in Him reveals that the meaning of time and the universe is found exclusively in Christ. So what we need every moment of every day is to live Christ (Phil. 1:21). We need to have Christ between us. Let Him be the bond of peace that holds everything together. Otherwise we are disoriented and we come apart. Christ not only holds my being together, He also holds my relationships together. This is the experiential benefit of all the fullness dwelling in Him.

This means He wants us to work through things in our relationships *until* we touch Him and settle our situations in Him. He will let you go "around the block" as many times as it takes for you to find out that He is waiting for you to experience Him. Let Him be your peace. Let the peace of Christ arbitrate in your heart (Col. 3:15). Do not let your thought, your insistence, or your controlling arbitrate. It is not trying to influence a person by your own manipulation, but it is letting Christ become your person and purity in your relationships. Let Him be your forgiveness. Let Him be grace to you so that you might give grace to others. Let the cross of Christ be the factor between you. Hold Him, the One who loves from the cross, the One who does not count our trespasses against us (2 Cor. 5:19), the One who does not calculate or "read the files" of others' failures, the One who washed everything away by His death and by the love that was demonstrated in that death. Now that same love has been poured out in our hearts and is resident in us and flows out of us toward one another. This is what holds us together. Again, we see why Paul said, "In Him all the fullness was pleased to dwell." It is because all the fullness, including time and the universe, finds its true meaning in Christ — He has the first place in time and in our moment-by-moment existence.

The church is included in all the fullness

All the fullness was pleased to dwell in Christ, and according to Colossians 1:18 this fullness includes the Body, the church. In other words, from the divine point of view the Body of Christ, organically joined to its Head, is a direct expression of the riches and fullness of the Head. Thus, all the fullness in verse 19 includes the church as the Body of Christ, the unique corporate expression of Himself. The church as part of all the fullness is pleased to dwell in Christ as her Head, life, and all. This is why the church as the Body is called "the Christ" in 1 Corinthians 12:12: "For as the body is one and has many members, but all the members of that one body, being many, are one body, so also is *the Christ*."

For us to separate the church from Christ can be a sign of ignorance and blindness. Do we know the kind of Christ who lives in us today? He is the Body-Christ. The kind of Christ who lives in us is the Head of His Body, the church. The Christ today in resurrection is a different kind of Christ from the Christ before the resurrection. The Christ in the four Gospels was limited to His one physical body. That was the individual Jesus of Nazareth. That was the Christ that Paul knew according to the flesh (2 Cor. 5:16). But now the kind of Christ who exists in this universe is the One joined organically to His church. He is a Christ who is Head of His Body, the church. He is a corporate Christ. He is an enlarged Christ. He is a Christ who regenerates our spirit and continues to indwell and fill every member so that the Body is vitally in union with the Head (Eph. 1:22-23).

The kind of Christ unfolded in the New Testament is a church-Christ. He is a Christ located in His members. Just as in the Gospels the Father was located in Jesus of Nazareth, so today Christ is located in His members. If Philip wanted to find the Father, he did not need to go any other place but to Jesus of Nazareth, because the Father was embodied in the Son. The Lord said to Philip, "He who has seen Me has seen the Father" (John 14:9). Do not dare separate the Father from Christ. If you do not have the Son, you do not have the Father.

Also, in the Epistles Paul tells us that the mystery of God is Christ (Col. 2:2). If you want to solve the mystery of God, look at Christ, because Christ is the embodiment of the Godhead. And in the same way, the mystery of Christ is the church, His Body (Eph. 3:4-6). The church is organically joined as life-members to the Head. The only kind of Christ we have today is this corporate Christ, the Christ who is expressed in His fullness, that is, in His Body, the church. Do you want to find Christ? You will find Him expressed in the members of the church. All the fullness was pleased to dwell in Him. So this fullness is now expressed in the church with Him as the Head, the One who is now filling all in all.

It is simply a lack of revelation that would separate the church from Christ. Paul did not separate them. When the Corinthian church was starting to be divided, Paul said, "Is

Christ divided?" He put church division in the category of Christ being divided. When we speak about the church — the church life, the practical serving, the riches of the church — we are talking about an enlarged Christ in whom all this fullness was pleased to dwell. Do you think we are talking about something different from Christ? Away with such a thought! It is not a method. It is not a way. It is not a person. It is not any *thing*. It is Christ expressed! And it is Christ expressed in the midst of all our imperfections and failures and offenses — all the things that have to do with all of us. But it is a Christ who has a fullness, including incarnation, human living, crucifixion, a death that solved all the problems, and resurrection. So now He can be all to all of us "broken-down shacks."

We are all broken down. We all have clutter in our hearts. We have old things stashed away in our "closets." We have junk. We have "extra baggage." We have ourselves. But now Christ has made home in us. He bought the property, and He has the deed to it. He owns me. I am His and He took me just as I am. And now I just turn over everything I have to Him: "Lord, only You can clean me up. Lord, wash me. Lord, fully cleanse me. Lord, purify my heart. I only know one thing — to call Your name, Jesus." When I say, "Jesus," He transmits all His fullness into me. And as He fills all His members, the church emerges as the very expression of Christ.

So what kind of Christ do you have? What kind of Christ do I have? Is it the Christ that Paul saw on the Damascus road? When the Lord said, "Saul, Saul, why are you persecuting Me?" notice how he answered. He said, "Who are You,

Lord?" At that point, Saul knew another kind of Christ — a Christ according to the flesh. He was in the old dimension of knowing Christ. He was asking, "What individual are You?" But the Lord said, "I am Jesus." He did not even say, "I am Christ," but "I am Jesus, whom you persecute." Paul had not been persecuting Jesus in an individual way, but he had been persecuting the members of Jesus! At that moment Paul had a revelation of the Body-Christ. To sin against the brothers was to sin against Christ.

Verses such as Matthew 25:40 also bring out this truth concerning the corporate Christ. Here the Lord says, "Inasmuch as you did it to one of the least of these My brethren, you did it to Me." This is the kind of Christ *after* the resurrection. That is why we love the church. To say "I love the church" means "I love Christ in His fullness. I love what He has done. I love where He lives. I love how He has transformed His organic members. I love what comes out from Him as the Head through each member. I love Him in all His fullness." This is the highest revelation of the church.

The nature and essence of God
is included in all the fullness

Ephesians 3:17-19 says, [17] "That Christ may make His home in your hearts through faith, that you, being rooted and grounded in love, [18] may be full of strength to apprehend with all the saints what the breadth and length and height and depth are [19] and to know the knowledge-surpassing love of Christ, that you may be filled unto all the fullness of God." Here "all the fullness of God" includes the love of Christ which passes knowledge. This knowledge-surpassing love is the nature and essence of God concentrated in Christ — "the love of God which is in Christ Jesus our Lord" (Rom. 8:39).

Ephesians 3:18 and 19 are connected by the conjunction "and." In Greek there are two ways to express "and." One is by using the word *kai* and the other is by using the word *te. Kai* is the conjunction normally used when you join two separate things together. However, when *te* is used, it means that what is being joined should not be separated in our thought. The things being joined are organically one thing. This is the case with these verses. They are joined by the conjunction *te.* So when verse 18 speaks of, "the breadth and length and height and depth," these are dimensions of something — that "something" is the knowledge-surpassing love of Christ in verse 19. So the specific meaning of the dimensions is *the dimensions of the love of Christ.* The Greek word for "and" shows us that the love of Christ is organically connected with the dimensions.

This knowledge-surpassing love is the divine standard of measurement in the church. Measurement is always happening in the church life. We are always being measured. How far does our love go? It is limited. It only goes so far. But in the divine life there is another kind of love, and its measurement goes all the way to the edge of the holy city, embracing *all* the saints. Again, Ephesians 3:18-19 shows that the vast dimensions are not, strictly speaking, the measurement of Christ in a general sense. That is not exactly the context here, although this is true. What is more accurate is that these dimensions refer to the knowledge-surpassing love of Christ. This means that the nature and essence of the love of God toward all the saints is included in all the fullness that was pleased to dwell in Christ.

When the church reaches this stage where there is the knowledge-surpassing love of Christ, this is the highest expression of being filled with all the fullness of God. This goes beyond our understanding. It is a church full of forgiveness, peace, and harmony. You do not get retaliation, but you get grace. You do not get an eye for an eye, and a tooth for a tooth. You may think that because of your mistakes you deserve to be put in your place, but you do not get that. You get Christ's love — a knowledge-surpassing love. And that love begins to fill the atmosphere of the church. And when this happens, it means the very essence and nature of God is embodied and perfected in His people. His essence flows between us. Then we have touched the highest stage of the expression of the fullness of God in this age. It is the presence of the knowledge-surpassing love of Christ that brings in the reality of being filled with all the fullness of God.

This indicates that the fullness of God is expressed to the universe when the Lord has so filled us up and has made home in our hearts to such an extent that He has the first place in all things. We let Him be the Lord over everything in our relationships in every dimension, and we are rooted and grounded in this knowledge-surpassing love of Christ. This is the main factor between us.

This is why the sense of fullness that we enjoy in the fellowship of the church is absolutely due to the present state of the love of God in our attitude toward one another. When the fullness is present, we are letting the Lord fill us, we are dropping offenses, gracing one another, being filled with God, not holding issues, not blaming, not looking at the church in a common way. We are not looking at the brothers and sisters from a natural point of view — calculating others' faults. What a low level to be on! Yes, I have faults and you have faults. Yet it would be an awful thing to be related to one another on the level of our faults. What if the Lord Jesus was related to us from the cross on the level of our faults and sins! This is why I love 2 Corinthians 5:19 — it tells us that He did not count our trespasses against us. This is the kind of love streaming from Calvary. This is Calvary love.

In the church life sometimes divisiveness comes in. It comes in through some kind of speaking about something that seems wrong. Then talk begins and it spreads like gangrene. An unhappy atmosphere comes in. When this takes place among any group of believers — be it denominational, non-denominational, or interdenominational — you have people who are back-biting and are fostering grudges. Eventually you end up with form, ritual, and deadness, and the young people leave, and there is no reality of the Spirit. So we are absolutely dependent upon all the fullness in Christ operating in our hearts to let the knowledge-surpassing love of Christ permeate us. Then we are not just loving *like* Christ, but we are loving *as* Christ. It is Christ Himself loving in us and through us.

This is how we are filled unto all the fullness of God. The fullness in the church is this knowledge-surpassing love of Christ being transmitted in our relationships with one another in the church. What a full expression of Christ! All this fullness, including all that is in the Godhead from eternity past to eternity future was pleased to dwell in Christ. It is all concentrated in Christ. And now what is concentrated in Christ, the Head, is expressed in the church, His Body. Praise the Lord!

Scripture Index

Old Testament

New Testament

Other Available Books:

by Bill Freeman

The Supplied Life

A Daily Devotional • 409 pages

The Cross and the Self

Describes the depths of the self-life while at the same time showing God's way of dealing with it • 321 pages

God's Unconditional Love

The nature of God's love revealed in the book of Hosea • 237 pages

The Kingdom Life

A study in the book of James showing the nature of the kingdom life in our daily life • 227 pages

How They Found Christ — in their own words

The personal testimonies of Augustine, Luther, Calvin, Bunyan, Guyon, Wesley, Edwards, Whitefield, Finney, Müller, Murray, H. W. Smith, H. Taylor, Spurgeon, A. B. Simpson, and W. Nee
Edited by Bill Freeman • 201 pages

Our Common Oneness

A study in the book of Romans revealing the common oneness of all believers regardless of backgrounds • 284 pages

Calling Upon the Name of the Lord

A study of the meaning, history, and basis of calling upon the Name of the Lord • 149 pages

Seeing and Feeling the Church

A study of Paul's prayers in the book of Ephesians • 138 pages

The Triune God in Experience

A study of the experiential emphasis on the Triune God throughout church history • 391 pages

Ordering Information:

You may use any of the following ways to order books from ***Ministry Publications***:

(1) **Write:** P.O. Box 28338
Scottsdale, AZ 85255

(2) **Phone:** (800) 573-4105

(3) **Email:** orders@thechristian.org

(4) **Website:** www.thechristian.org